apples

apples

Louise Mackaness

photography by David Loftus

conran OCTOPUS

Starters

Dolcelatte, Ricotta, Prosciutto and Thyme Tart

Preparation time: 1 hour 30 minutes, plus 40 minutes chilling time
Serves 6–8

300 g/10 oz ready-to-roll shortcrust pastry
2 tablespoons olive oil
4 large banana shallots, peeled and thinly sliced
1 large garlic clove, peeled and finely crushed
250 g/8 oz ricotta cheese
2 tablespoons fresh thyme leaves
2 tablespoons finely chopped chervil
3 large organic eggs, plus 2 yolks
250 ml/8 oz double cream
freshly ground black pepper and sea salt
200 g/7 oz Dolcelatte cheese
4 thin slices of prosciutto
1 apple (such as Cox's), cored and sliced
green salad, to serve

Preheat the oven to 200°C/400°F/gas mark 6.

Roll out the pastry on a lightly floured work surface until it is large enough to fit a 24 cm/9½ in fluted, deep-sided, loose-bottomed tart tin. Line the tin with the pastry, pressing down gently, and prick the bottom with a fork. Chill for about 40 minutes, then line with some greaseproof paper and fill with baking beans.

Put the chilled pastry case in the centre of the oven and bake for 20 minutes. Remove, take out the greaseproof paper and baking beans and return to the oven for 5 minutes to dry out the bottom. Remove from the oven and reduce the temperature to 180°C/350°F/gas mark 4.

Meanwhile, heat the oil in a frying pan and gently fry the shallots and garlic for about 10 minutes or until soft, golden and melting. Add the ricotta and herbs and cook for a further 2 minutes.

Crack the eggs into a jug, add the cream, whisk lightly and season. Spoon the onion mixture into the pastry case and pour in the cream. Dot with the Dolcelatte, then lay the prosciutto and apple slices on top. Bake in the oven for 25 minutes or until risen and golden.

Serve hot or warm with a green salad.

Camembert and Apple Filo

Preparation time: 30 minutes, plus 20 minutes
chilling time
Serves 4

1 apple (such as Braeburn), peeled, cored and sliced
juice of 1 lemon
5 sheets of filo pastry (about 28 x 16 cm/11 x 6½ in)
25 g/1 oz unsalted butter, melted
1 x 250 g/8 oz ripe Camembert
freshly ground black pepper
green salad, to serve

Toss the apple slices in the lemon juice.

Place one sheet of filo on to a lightly greased baking sheet, brush with butter, place another on top of that and also brush with butter. Place the next sheet 90° to the last sheet, so it forms a cross, brush with butter and place one more sheet on top and brush with butter.

Place half the apple slices in the middle of the filo cross, sit the Camembert on top and then cover the top with the remaining apples. Season with a little black pepper.

Fold the filo over the Camembert and brush the parcel with melted butter. Brush the last sheet of filo with butter and rip or cut into four strips, then crumple on top of the parcel to decorate.

Place in the fridge for 20 minutes, or until needed.

Preheat the oven to 180°C/350°F/gas mark 4.

Bake the filo parcel in the oven for 20 minutes, or until it is golden. Place on a warm plate and let everyone help themselves. Serve with a green salad.

Apple Rarebit

Preparation time: 25 minutes
Serves 4

50 g/2 oz unsalted butter
½ tablespoon caster sugar
1 green apple (such as Granny Smith), quartered,
    cored and thickly sliced
4 thick slices of day-old white bread
400 g/13 oz strong Cheddar, grated
100 ml/3½ fl oz sweet cider
1 tablespoon English mustard
1 organic egg yolk
freshly ground black pepper

Set a frying pan over a medium heat, add the butter and when it has melted, sprinkle in the caster sugar. Once the sugar has dissolved, turn up the heat and add the apple slices. Fry the apples on both sides until they take on a golden colour. Remove them from the pan and keep warm until needed.

Toast both sides of the bread very lightly in either a toaster or under a hot grill.

Place the cheese, cider, mustard and egg yolk in a pan over a gentle heat, stirring regularly. Once the cheese has melted and you have a smooth mixture, remove the pan from the heat and set aside to cool.

Spoon the mixture over the lightly toasted bread and grill under a medium to hot grill until golden. Scatter the fried apple slices over the rarebit, season with freshly ground black pepper and serve immediately.

Pork, Apple and Sage Ravioli with Sage Butter

Preparation time: 55 minutes
Serves 4

100 g/3½ oz ghee or clarified unsalted butter (see right)
about 20 sage leaves
1 tablespoon olive oil
½ onion, peeled and finely chopped
1 apple (such as Cox's), peeled, cored and finely chopped
1 tablespoon fresh sage leaves, finely chopped
2 good pork sausages, skins removed
freshly ground black pepper and sea salt
24 fresh lasagne sheets
1 large organic egg, lightly beaten
about 25 g/1 oz semolina

Heat the ghee or clarified butter in a small pan, add the whole sage leaves and cook for 3–4 minutes, or until the leaves look crispy. Set aside and keep warm.

Heat the oil in a frying pan and add the onions. Fry for about 5 minutes, or until soft and melting. Add the apple and fry for a further 4–5 minutes. Remove from the heat and add the chopped sage, sausage meat, and seasoning and mix well to combine.

Cut out twenty four 8 cm/3 in rounds from the lasagne sheets. Lightly dust a sheet of greaseproof paper with semolina and place the pasta rounds on it. Place 1–2 heaped teaspoons of mixture in the middle of 12 of the rounds and brush each edge with beaten egg. Place the remaining rounds on top and pinch the edges firmly together to make 12 ravioli.

Bring a large deep-sided pan of salted water to the boil, add the pasta and cook for 4–5 minutes or until al dente. Drain the ravioli well and toss in the sage butter. Serve on warm plates, sprinkle with black pepper and garnish with the sage leaves.

Chicken Liver and Calvados Pâté

Preparation time: 40 minutes, plus chilling time
Serves 4–6

125 g/5 oz unsalted butter
1 tablespoon olive oil
1 onion, peeled and roughly chopped
1 large garlic clove, peeled and finely chopped
1 tablespoon finely chopped fresh rosemary
450 g/14½ oz chicken livers, chopped
200 ml/7 fl oz Calvados
100 ml/3½ fl oz double cream
freshly ground black pepper
1–2 sprigs rosemary, to garnish

This recipe includes instructions for clarifying butter, though, if you prefer, you can buy it ready-made. Clarified butter is also known as ghee.

To make clarified butter, melt 75 g/3 oz of the butter in a small saucepan over a medium heat, then pour it through some muslin into a jug.

Heat the oil and half the remaining butter in a frying pan. Add the onion, garlic and rosemary and fry for 10 minutes or until the onion is soft and melting. Add the chicken livers and fry for a further 5 minutes. Pour in the Calvados, bring to the boil and allow it to bubble until the liquid has reduced by half. Remove the pan from the heat and set the mixture aside to cool.

Put the remaining butter and the double cream in a food processor and whizz until light and fluffy. Add the cooled liver mixture and whizz in short bursts until it forms a smooth paste. Take care not to overblend or the pâté will become sticky. Season with some pepper to taste.

Spoon the pâté into a serving bowl, then melt the clarified butter and pour over the top. Submerge the rosemary sprigs in the butter and chill until set.

Cheddar and Cider Soufflé

Preparation time: 55 minutes
Serves 6

2 tablespoons freshly grated Parmesan cheese
25 g/1 oz unsalted butter, plus a little extra for greasing
50 g/2 oz plain flour
75 ml/3 fl oz full-fat milk
75 ml/3 fl oz cider
5 organic egg yolks and 4 egg whites
250 g/8 oz mature organic Cheddar cheese, grated
freshly ground black pepper
salad, to serve

Preheat the oven to 190°C/375°F/gas mark 5. Grease six 150 ml/¼ pint ramekin dishes and sprinkle Parmesan in base of each one.

Put the butter in a saucepan and melt slowly. Add the flour and cook for 2 minutes over a medium heat. Slowly whisk in the milk and cider, stirring continuously until the sauce has thickened. Remove from the heat and cool slightly.

Beat the egg yolks into the sauce and add 200 g/7 oz of the Cheddar, stirring well. Season with black pepper.

Whisk the egg whites in a clean, grease-free bowl until they form peaks. Using a metal spoon, carefully fold the egg whites into the cheese sauce. Divide the mixture between the six ramekins, sprinkle the remaining Cheddar on top and bake for about 20 minutes, or until well risen and golden.

Remove and serve immediately with salad.

Grilled Haloumi with Apple Chilli Salsa Verde

Preparation time: 25 minutes
Serves 4

2 handfuls of fresh flat-leaf parsley
zest and juice of 1 lemon
3 garlic cloves, peeled and crushed
1 small chilli, halved, deseeded and chopped
2 tablespoons capers
½ apple, peeled, cored and finely grated
extra virgin olive oil
freshly ground black pepper
500 g/1 lb haloumi cheese

To make the salsa, put the parsley, lemon zest, garlic, chilli and capers in a food processor and whizz until finely chopped. Transfer to a bowl, add the lemon juice, apple and enough oil to make the salsa moist. Season with black pepper to taste. Cover until needed.

Preheat the grill to a high heat. Slice the haloumi – you should have enough for 3–4 slices per person – and spread each slice with a little of the salsa. Grill for 5 minutes or until golden, then turn over, spread the other side with salsa and repeat. Serve with a mixed salad.

Cottage Cheese and Fresh Fruit Salad with Coriander Dressing

Preparation time: 25 minutes
Serves 4

dressing
small bunch of fresh coriander
100 ml/3½ fl oz olive oil
juice of 1 lemon
freshly ground black pepper and sea salt

salad
50 g/2 oz pumpkin seeds
50 g/2 oz sunflower seeds
450 g/14½ oz tub low-fat cottage cheese
4 plums, quartered and stoned
8 fresh pineapple slices
1 crunchy apple (such as Pink Lady), cored and sliced
2 kiwifruit, peeled and sliced
1 papaya, peeled and sliced
1 large white peach, halved and sliced
large bag of mixed salad

To make the dressing, put the coriander, olive oil and lemon juice in a food processor and whizz until finely chopped. Season to taste and set aside.

Preheat the grill to medium. Spread out the pumpkin seeds and sunflower seeds on a large baking sheet and place under the grill, stirring the seeds occasionally until lightly toasted. Leave to cool.

Divide the cottage cheese among four large, shallow soup bowls. Add a mixture of fruit and salad leaves to each bowl. Sprinkle over the lightly toasted seeds, drizzle with the dressing and serve.

Apple and Butternut Squash Soup

Preparation time: 1 hour 5 minutes
Serves 6

30 ml/1 fl oz olive oil
2 onions, peeled and roughly chopped
1–2 garlic cloves, peeled and crushed
2 teaspoons ground coriander
300 ml/½ pint good white wine
1 kg/2 lb butternut squash flesh, roughly chopped
1 large potato, peeled and roughly chopped
1.2 litres/2 pints fresh chicken or vegetable stock
2 large apples (such as Braeburn), peeled, cored and roughly chopped
freshly ground black pepper and sea salt
Dried Apple Rings (see page 84) and flat-leaf parsley, to garnish

Put the oil in a large saucepan and set over a medium heat. Add the onions and garlic and fry for about 10 minutes, or until soft and melting. Add the coriander and fry for a further minute. Add the wine and boil until it is reduced by half. Add the butternut squash, potato and stock. Bring back to the boil, then reduce to a simmer and cover. Simmer for 30 minutes, then add the apples. Cook for a further 15 minutes, then remove from the heat. Leave to cool.

Working in batches if necessary, put the soup in a food processor and whizz until smooth. Transfer to a clean saucepan, warm through and season to taste.

Serve in warm soup bowls, garnished with dried apple rings and flat-leaf parsley.

Cider and Onion Soup

Preparation time: 1 hour
Serves 6

50 g/2 oz unsalted butter
3 tablespoons olive oil
1 kg/2 lb onions, peeled, halved and thinly sliced
2 garlic cloves
500 ml/17 fl oz fresh chicken or vegetable stock
500 ml/17 fl oz medium dry cider
freshly ground black pepper and sea salt

Melt the butter in a large saucepan over a medium heat.
Add the oil, onions and garlic and fry, stirring from time
to time, for 30 minutes, or until they are soft, melting and
golden. (If the mixture starts to stick to the bottom of the
pan, add a little water.) Pour the stock and cider into the
saucepan, increase the heat to high and bring to the boil.
Continue to boil, uncovered, for 4–5 minutes, then season
with salt and pepper to taste.

To serve, pour into warm soup bowls.

Apple Vichyssoise

Preparation time: 45 minutes
Serves 6

4 large potatoes, peeled and roughly chopped
5 celery sticks, trimmed and roughly chopped
4 apples (such as Empire), peeled, cored and
   roughly chopped
750 ml/1¼ pints fresh chicken or vegetable stock
20 g/¾ oz unsalted butter
2 teaspoons curry powder
250 ml/8 fl oz double cream
freshly ground black pepper and sea salt
very finely sliced red and green apple skin, to garnish

Put the potatoes, celery and apples in a saucepan, pour
over the stock and bring to the boil. Cover and simmer for
20 minutes, or until the vegetables and apple are tender.
Add the butter and curry powder to the pan and simmer
for a further 4 minutes. Leave to cool slightly.

Working in batches, if necessary, transfer the mixture to a
food processor and whizz until smooth. Pour into a large jug,
and add the cream. Season to taste, then chill.

To serve, pour the soup into chilled soup bowls and
garnish with the fine strips of red and green apple skin.

Gravadlax with Mustard and Calvados Mayonnaise

Preparation time: 35 minutes, plus 48 hours curing time
Serves 6–8

gravadlax
2 wild salmon fillets
250 g/8 oz caster sugar
1 teaspoon ground fennel seeds
1 teaspoon ground black peppercorns
5 tablespoons finely chopped fresh dill
500 g/1 lb pack Maldon sea salt

mayonnaise
2 organic egg yolks
1 tablespoon Dijon mustard
2 teaspoons Calvados
300 ml/½ pint light olive oil
1 tablespoon finely chopped dill
freshly ground black pepper and sea salt

Line a roasting tray with cling film. Remove any large bones from the salmon, then, using tweezers, carefully pull out the tiny bones. Mix together the sugar, fennel seeds, black peppercorns, dill and half the salt. Put 1 salmon fillet, skin side down, on the clingfilm in the roasting tray. Sprinkle the dill mixture over the fillet. Put the other fillet on top, skin side up, and press together. Cover with the remaining salt, making sure that the sides of the fish are well coated with salt. Cover and chill for 48 hours.

To make the mayonnaise, put the egg yolks, mustard and Calvados in a food processor and whizz for 1 minute. Slowly add the oil, a little at a time, with the motor running all the time. Transfer to a bowl and stir in 1 tablespoon of boiling water and the dill and season to taste. Cover and chill until needed.

To serve, brush all the salt off the salmon, slice thinly and serve with the mayonnaise.

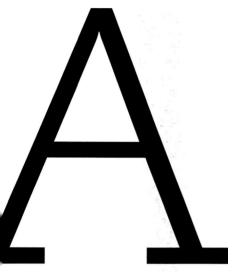cold starter is a great idea for busy cooks as it can be prepared in advance and served at the last minute. Why make life any harder than necessary? Many of the recipes in this chapter, such as Pork, Apple and Sage Ravioli with Sage Butter are also ideal as a light lunch.

The range of soups in which apple can be used to different effect shows just how versatile this fruit can be – soothing in Apple and Butternut Squash Soup, yet light and refreshing in Apple Vichyssoise. Serve them with crunchy breads to dip in the soup and then wipe round the bowl to soak up any precious last few drops.

If you make one of the salads, such as Prawn and Apple Salad, you'll notice how important the shape and texture of the apple is to the overall effect. Try chopping or dicing them to different sizes and see what a difference it makes to the salad.

Smoked Chicken, Apple, Chicory and Walnut Salad

Preparation time: 15 minutes
Serves 4

dressing
6 tablespoons olive oil
2 tablespoons white wine vinegar
1 tablespoon wholegrain mustard
1 tablespoon finely chopped fresh tarragon
freshly ground black pepper and sea salt

salad
50 g/2 oz walnut halves
2 smoked chicken breasts
1 green apple (such as Golden Delicious),
    quartered, cored and sliced
1 red apple (such as Red Delicious),
    quartered, cored and sliced
juice of 1 lemon
2 chicory heads
bunch of watercress

To make the dressing, put all the ingredients in a jam jar. Screw the lid on and shake hard until the ingredients are thoroughly mixed. Season to taste, then set aside.

Preheat the grill to medium. Spread the nuts on a baking sheet and place under the grill, stirring the nuts occasionally until they are lightly toasted. Leave to cool.

Slice the chicken breasts and put in a large salad bowl. Toss the apples in the lemon juice and add to the bowl. Trim the chicory, tear off the leaves and add to the bowl, then add the watercress and nuts. Toss in the dressing and season.

Prawn and Apple Salad

Preparation time: 10 minutes
Serves 4

450 g/14½ oz cooked and peeled prawns
½ fennel head, finely sliced
1 celery heart, washed and finely sliced
handful of fresh dill, finely chopped
handful of fresh flat-leaf parsley, chopped
175 g/6 oz seedless green grapes, halved
2 green apples (such as Granny Smith), quartered, cored
    and roughly chopped
250 ml/8 fl oz fresh mayonnaise
juice of 1 lemon
freshly ground black pepper
watercress, to serve (optional)

Gently mix the peeled prawns, fennel, sliced celery, dill, parsley, grape halves, chopped apples and mayonnaise together in a large bowl. Squeeze over the lemon juice and season with some freshly ground black pepper.

Spoon the mixture on to four plates. You could add a few sprigs of watercress as a garnish, if you like too.

Main Courses

Chicken in Cider Sauce

Preparation time: 1 hour 10 minutes
Serves 4

2 tablespoons olive oil
1 onion, peeled and finely chopped
2 apples (such as Cox's), peeled, cored and roughly chopped
100 g/3½ oz plain flour
freshly ground black pepper and sea salt
4 chicken pieces
450 ml/¾ pint dry cider
2 heaped tablespoons crème fraîche

Preheat the oven to 180°C/350°F/gas mark 4.
Set a frying pan over a medium heat and add 1 tablespoon of the oil. Add the onion and fry for 8–10 minutes until soft and melting. Halfway through, add the apples to the pan. Remove the onions and apples from the pan and transfer to an ovenproof casserole dish.

Season the flour with a good grinding of salt and pepper and dust the chicken pieces in it. Wipe the frying plan clean with some kitchen paper and heat the remaining oil over a medium heat. Add half the chicken to the pan, skin side down, and fry until the skin is golden. Turn over, seal on all sides and remove. Repeat with the remaining chicken pieces. Add all the chicken and any cooking juices to the onions and apples in the casserole dish. Pour the cider into the dish, cover and place in the oven for about 45 minutes, or until the juices run clear from the chicken when pierced with a skewer.

Remove the chicken from the casserole dish, cover with kitchen foil and keep warm. Using a hand-held blender, purée the onion and cider mixture. Add the crème fraîche and season with salt and pepper to taste. Return the chicken to the sauce and serve immediately.

Sticky Apple-glazed Chicken Wings

Preparation time: 35 minutes
Makes 16 wings

300 ml/½ pint clear apple juice
4 tablespoons tomato ketchup
2 tablespoons maple syrup
1 tablespoon Worcestershire sauce
2 garlic cloves, peeled and finely chopped
juice of 1 lemon
freshly ground black pepper and sea salt
16 organic chicken wings
chopped chives, to garnish

Preheat the grill to the medium high setting.

Pour the apple juice into a saucepan and boil until reduced to about 75 ml/3 fl oz.

Mix together the reduced apple juice, ketchup, maple syrup, Worcestershire sauce, garlic, lemon juice and seasoning.

Place the chicken wings onto a baking sheet and liberally brush the wings all over with the sauce.

Place the wings under the grill and cook for 20 minutes, turning and basting with more sauce occasionally, until the wings are crispy and golden brown. The wings can also be barbecued in the same way. Serve hot.

Moroccan Chicken

Preparation time: 2 hours 30 minutes, plus
soaking time
Serves 6

200 g/7 oz semi-dried apricots, halved
100 g/3½ oz dried figs, halved
100 g/3½ oz dried dates, halved
300 ml/½ pint clear apple juice, warmed
6 chicken pieces
2–4 tablespoons sunflower oil
15 g/½ oz unsalted butter
2 red onions, peeled and sliced
1–2 garlic cloves, peeled
2–3 cm/¾–1¼ in fresh ginger, peeled and finely grated
2 teaspoons ground cumin
1 teaspoon ground coriander
3 preserved lemons, rinsed, halved and seeded
200 g/7 oz (drained weight) green olives, pitted
600 ml/1 pint chicken stock
freshly ground black pepper and sea salt
small bunch of coriander, roughly chopped
couscous, to serve

Preheat the oven to 160°C/325°F/gas mark 3.

Put the apricots, figs and dates in a bowl and pour over the warm apple juice. Leave to soak for about 2 hours; the fruit will soften as they absorb the juice.

Season the chicken skin with salt. Heat half the sunflower oil in a frying pan and, once hot, add the chicken in batches, and fry until the skin is brown.

Meanwhile, melt the butter in a large non-stick ovenproof casserole dish, add the remaining sunflower oil, onions and garlic, and fry for about 6 minutes. Stir in the ginger and ground spices and fry for 2 minutes.

Add the chicken pieces, skin side up, then add the preserved lemons, olives and soaked fruits plus the juice. Pour in the chicken stock. Bring to the boil, cover the dish and cook in the oven for about 1½ hours, or until the chicken juices run clear when the thickest parts are pierced with the point of a sharp knife. Spoon off any fat from the surface, season with salt and pepper to taste and add the coriander.

Serve on a bed of couscous.

Roast Duck with Port and Apple Brandy Sauce

Preparation time: 1 hour 50 minutes
Serves 4

1 oven-ready duck
1 onion, peeled and halved
handful of marjoram
2 apples, (such as Golden Russet) halved
freshly ground black pepper and sea salt
2 tablespoons apple brandy

sauce
100 g/3½ oz redcurrant jelly
200 ml/7 fl oz good port
100 ml/3½ fl oz apple brandy
julienne peel and juice of 1 orange
juice of ½ lemon

Preheat the oven to 200°C/400°F/gas mark 6.

Season the skin of the duck and fill the cavity with the onion, marjoram and apples. Place the duck, on its back in a roasting tray and season the under side. Place the duck in the oven and roast for 30 minutes. Turn the oven down to 180°C/350°F/gas mark 4, remove the duck from the oven and turn it the right way up. Baste the duck with the juices from the tray and pour over the brandy. Return to the oven for 1 hour, or until the duck is cooked through.

While the duck is cooking, place all the ingredients for the sauce in a saucepan. Heat gently until the redcurrant jelly has dissolved, bring to the boil and boil for 2–4 minutes. Keep warm until needed.

Once the duck is cooked, leave it to rest for 5 minutes. Remove the fat from the roasting tray and pour the duck juice into the sauce. Serve with the duck.

Normandy Pheasant

Preparation time: 1 hour 15 minutes
Serves 2–3

100 g/3½ oz unsalted butter
1 oven-ready pheasant
freshly ground black pepper and sea salt
500 g/1 lb apples (such as Braeburn), peeled and sliced
150 ml/¼ pint double cream
75 ml/3 fl oz Calvados

Preheat the oven to 180°C/350°F/gas mark 4.

Smear 75 g/3 oz of the butter over the breast of the pheasant and season well. Take a casserole dish that is large enough to hold the pheasant snuggly and grease with the remaining butter and season with salt and pepper.

Lay half the apples in a layer in the dish and sit the pheasant on top. Cover the pheasant with the remaining apples and pour the cream and Calvados evenly over the top. Cover the dish tightly and cook in the oven for 1 hour, or until the juices of the pheasant run clear when pierced with a skewer.

Quail with Juniper Berries and Apple

Preparation time: 1 hour 5 minutes
Serves 2

100 g/3½ oz unsalted butter
4 oven-ready quails
50 g/2 oz plain flour
1 small apple (such as Royal Gala), quartered and cored
1 small unwaxed lemon, quartered
8 sprigs of lemon thyme
3 tablespoons olive oil
150 g/5 oz chestnut mushrooms
75 ml/3 fl oz apple brandy
6–8 juniper berries, freshly ground
½ bottle good white wine
freshly ground black pepper and sea salt

Preheat the oven to 190°C/375°F/gas mark 5.

Melt half the butter in a heavy-based frying pan. Season the flour with a few grinds of salt and pepper, then dust it over the quails.

Heat a large frying pan over a medium heat, add a tablespoon of olive oil and, when hot, brown the quails on all sides. Remove the birds from the pan and transfer them to a roasting tray.

Fill the cavity of each quail with an apple quarter, a lemon quarter and a few spring of lemon thyme. Spread the remaining soft butter over the quail. Roast the quail in the preheated oven for 20–25 minutes, or until they are cooked. When pierced with a skewer, the juices from the quail breast should run clear. Take care not to overcook them, however, because the quail will become dry.

Add the remaining oil to the frying pan and add the chestnut mushrooms. Gently fry them over a low heat for 5 minutes, then add the apple brandy, juniper berries and wine. Increase the heat to high and allow the sauce to bubble away until it has reduced by half. The liquor should take on a thick syrupy consistency. Taste and season with salt and pepper as necessary.

Long, slow cooking is the key to most roasts and stews. The gentle heat allows the flavours to develop and the meat to become beautifully tender. Cider and Pork Stew, is just such a dish and although it takes a few hours to cook, the stew only needs an occasional stir as it lazily bubbles away in the oven.

Game such as quail might not be something that you would usually cook, but don't be afraid to try something different. Here the bitter flavour of juniper berries, known so well to gin drinkers, mellows during the cooking process to lend the quail a deliciously mellow, spicy background taste.

And don't forget to feed the eye as well as the palate. In Skate Wings with Apple and Pineapple Salsa, the bright red of the apple skin is integral to the appeal of dish.

Pork Steaks with Apple and Cheese Sauce

Preparation time: 1 hour 5 minutes
Serves 4

4 x 175 g/6 oz pork steaks
freshly ground black pepper and sea salt
1 tablespoon olive oil
350 g/11½ oz shallots, peeled and halved
2 garlic cloves, peeled and finely chopped
1 large cooking apple (such as Bramley), peeled,
   cored and roughly chopped
400 ml/14 fl oz dry white wine
350 ml/12 fl oz double cream
250 g/8 oz Gorgonzola cheese, crumbled
25 g/1 oz Parmesan cheese, freshly grated

Preheat the oven to 180°C/350°F/gas mark 4.

Season the pork steaks with some freshly ground black pepper and sea salt.

Heat a heavy-based frying pan over a medium heat and add the olive oil. Place the pork steaks in the hot pan and fry them on both sides until golden brown. Remove the steaks from the pan and place them in a casserole dish. Cover and keep warm while you prepare the sauce.

Add the shallots and garlic to the frying pan and fry gently for 6–8 minutes. Add the apple to the shallots and garlic and fry for a further 2–3 minutes.

Pour in the wine and bring the mixture to the boil. Allow the sauce to bubble away until the wine has reduced in volume by half.

Using the back of a fork, break up the apple. Stir in the double cream and bring to the boil. Lower the heat and simmer until the sauce becomes thick and syrupy.

Stir in the Gorgonzola cheese – it will quickly melt into the sauce. Season with some freshly ground black pepper. Pour the sauce over the pork in the casserole dish and sprinkle with the Parmesan cheese. Place in the oven for 15 minutes, or until the pork is cooked through. Serve immediately.

Cider and Pork Stew

Preparation time: 4 hours
Serves 4–6

450 g/14½ oz shoulder of pork, trimmed and cubed
freshly ground black pepper and sea salt
4–6 tablespoons sunflower oil
4 red peppers, halved and deseeded
2 yellow peppers, halved and deseeded
3 red onions, peeled, halved and thinly sliced
1 clove garlic, peeled and crushed
1–2 teaspoons cayenne pepper
1–2 tablespoons paprika
4 ripe plum tomatoes, skinned and chopped
1 x 400 g/13 oz tin of chopped plum tomatoes
2–3 sprigs of thyme
150 ml/¼ pint fresh chicken or vegetable stock
300 ml/½ pint dry cider

Preheat the grill to high, and the oven to 140°C/275°F/gas mark 1.

Season the meat with pepper and salt. Heat half the oil in a large frying pan over a medium heat and fry the pork cubes in batches until golden on all sides. Transfer to a casserole dish.

Place the pepper halves, skin side up, on a grill pan and grill until their skins are very black. Remove and place in a bowl, covered with clingfilm, until cool. Slide the skins off the peppers, slice the flesh and add to the casserole dish.

Wipe the frying pan clean. Add the remaining oil and add the onions and garlic. Fry for 10 minutes until very soft, taking care not to let them get too brown. If they start to stick, add a little water. Add the cayenne and paprika and cook for 2–3 minutes, then add the tomatoes and thyme and cook over a medium heat for 15–20 minutes, or until the sauce is thick. Stir the mixture from time to time.

Pour the tomato mixture, stock and cider over the pork and peppers. Mix well and season with pepper. Cover and place in the oven for 3 hours, or until the meat is tender. Check from time to time and give the stew a stir. If it looks a little dry add some water. Serve hot.

Loin of Pork with Apple and Mustard Sauce

Preparation time: 1 hour 45 minutes
Serves 4

pork
1 kg/2 lb boned pork loin joint, with skin
1 tablespoon cumin seeds
1 tablespoon coriander seeds
freshly ground black pepper and sea salt
4–6 tablespoons goose fat

apple and mustard sauce
150 ml/¼ pint apple purée
100 ml/3½ fl oz apple juice
3–4 tablespoons grainy mustard
285 ml/9 fl oz double cream

Preheat the oven to 200°C/400°F/gas mark 6.

Using a sharp knife, score the rind of the joint in a criss-cross pattern; this will help the skin to become beautifully crisp when roasted.

Heat a small frying pan and drop in the cumin seeds and coriander seeds and dry-fry them for 2–3 minutes. Remove them from the pan and lightly crush using a pestle and mortar (or a small bowl and the end of a rolling pin). Mix the crushed spices with 1 tablespoon of sea salt.

Melt 2 tablespoons of the goose fat in a frying pan set over a medium heat. Once hot, add the pork, skin side down, and fry for about 5 minutes, or until the rind starts to change colour. It will spit like mad, so watch your hands. Seal both sides of the pork, then transfer to a roasting tray and cover with the remaining goose fat.

Rub the spice and sea salt mixture over the rind and roast in the oven for about 20 minutes. Reduce the temperature to 180°C/350°F/gas mark 4 and roast for a further 45 minutes, or until the juices run clear from the pork when the thickest part of the meat is pierced with a skewer. Transfer the pork loin to a warm plate, cover with foil and leave to rest while you prepare the sauce. Reserve the cooking juices left in the roasting tray.

To make the sauce, put the apple purée, apple juice, mustard and double cream in a small saucepan. Stir them together and gently warm through over a low heat. Add the reserved meat juices to the sauce and season with salt and freshly ground black pepper to taste.

Carve the pork and serve immediately with the warm apple and mustard sauce.

Pork, Chorizo and Apple Kebabs

Preparation time: 45 minutes, plus 1 hour
marinating time
Serves 6

12 wooden skewers
75 ml/3 fl oz good olive oil, plus extra for greasing
4 garlic cloves, peeled and finely crushed
juice of 2 lemons
2 tablespoons chopped fresh parsley
600 g/1¼ lb pork fillet, trimmed and cut into cubes
400 g/13 oz raw chorizo sausage
2–3 red apples (such as Red Delicious), cored
1 red onion, cut into 12 wedges
freshly ground black pepper and sea salt

dressing
150 ml/¼ pint plain yogurt
1 tablespoon olive oil
large pinch of ground cumin
large pinch of ground coriander
squeeze of lemon juice

First make the dressing, mix the yogurt, olive oil, cumin, coriander and lemon juice together in a bowl.

Fill a wide bowl with water and soak the wooden skewers for 30 minutes to prevent them catching fire during the cooking process.

Mix the olive oil, garlic, lemon juice and parsley together in a bowl. Add the pork cubes, stir well to coat in the marinade, cover and leave to marinate for at least 1 hour.

Chop the chorizo sausage into chunks about the same size as the pork cubes. Cut the apples into 24 wedges. Assemble the kebabs by alternating pieces of the pork, chorizo, apple and onion on each skewer. Season with salt and pepper.

Place a griddle pan over a high heat and lightly brush with oil. When the pan is hot, lay three kebabs on the pan and cook them for about 10–15 minutes. Turn the kebabs to cook them evenly on each side and brush with marinade halfway through. Once they are cooked, put the kebabs in a warm oven while you cook the remaining kebabs. They also taste great cooked on a barbecue. Serve with the dressing.

Pork and Apple Sweet and Sour

Preparation time: 1 hour 25 minutes
Serve 6

4 x 175 g/6 oz pork steaks
freshly ground black pepper and sea salt
2–3 tablespoons oil
2 red onions, peeled, halved and thinly sliced
1 garlic clove, peeled and finely crushed
1 red pepper, halved, deseeded, skinned and sliced
1 yellow pepper, halved, deseeded, skinned and sliced
1 red chilli, halved, deseeded and finely chopped
2 tablespoons tomato purée
2–3 heaped tablespoons mango chutney
1 tablespoon balsamic vinegar
250 ml/8 fl oz clear apple juice
pinch of brown sugar
1 small pineapple, peeled, cored and cubed
rice, to serve

Season the pork steaks with salt and pepper and cut them into bite-sized chunks. Heat a large non-stick frying pan and dry-fry the pork cubes over a high heat for 2–4 minutes until every side is golden brown. You may need to do this in batches to ensure that the pan does not become too crowded. Transfer the meat to an ovenproof dish and keep warm.

Reduce the heat, add the oil to the pan and fry the onions and garlic until soft and melting. Add the red and yellow peppers, chilli and tomato purée and fry for 2–4 minutes. Add the chutney, balsamic vinegar, apple juice and a pinch of brown sugar and cook for 5 minutes.

Add the pineapple flesh to the pork. Pour the sauce over the pork and place in the oven for 30 minutes, or until the meat is cooked through. Season with salt and pepper to taste. Serve immediately on a bed of rice.

Pork and Apple Stroganoff

Preparation time: 30 minutes
Serves 6

600 g/1¼ lb pork fillet, trimmed and cut into thin strips
freshly ground black pepper and sea salt
2 teaspoons Worcestershire sauce
5 tablespoons sunflower oil
50 g/2 oz unsalted butter
2 onions, peeled and thinly sliced
300 g/10 oz chestnut mushrooms, trimmed and finely sliced
150 g/5 oz cooking apples (such as Bramley), thickly sliced
2 tablespoons tomato purée
4 tablespoons Calvados
575 ml/18 fl oz soured cream
juice of 1 lemon
pinch of paprika

Put the pork in a bowl and season with salt, black pepper and Worcestershire sauce. Set a large heavy-bottomed frying pan over a high heat. Add 3 tablespoons of oil and, when very hot, add half the pork and stir-fry briskly until lightly browned. Remove the meat to a bowl, then add the rest of the oil to the pan and cook the remaining meat in the same way and transfer to the bowl.

Reduce the heat and melt the butter in the pan. Add the onions and fry gently until soft and melting. Add the mushrooms and apples and fry briskly until tender. Stir in the tomato purée and cook for 2 minutes. Return the pork and any juices to the pan and pour over the Cognac. Set alight at once and shake the pan until the alcohol has burnt itself off, then stir in the soured cream. Heat through, then stir in the lemon juice, season to taste and sprinkle with a little paprika.

Serve immediately.

Confit of Pork with Roasted Apples

Preparation time: 2 hours 45 minutes, plus 2 days
chilling time
Serves 4

1 kg/2 lb rolled boned pork belly, skin removed
700 g/1 lb 6 oz canned goose fat (*graisse d'oie*)
1 teaspoon ground cloves
1 teaspoon ground cinnamon
1 star anise, crushed to a powder
4 fresh bay leaves, torn
6 garlic clove, skin on
100 g/3½ oz sea salt
freshly ground black pepper
4 red apples (such as Cox's) halved and cored
steamed green vegetables, to serve

Place the belly of pork into a saucepan, cover with boiling
water and boil for 3–5 minutes. Drain and pat dry.

Melt the goose fat with the cloves, cinnamon, star anise,
bay leaves, garlic, salt and black pepper over a low heat in
a thick-bottomed pan just large enough to fit the pork.
Dry the pork, then put it in the warm fat, making sure
that it is completely immersed. Cover and simmer gently
for 2 hours. It is cooked when a wooden skewer can pass
through with no resistance. Remove the pork from the fat
and leave both to cool.

When the fat is cold, put the pork in a sterilized porcelain,
earthenware or glass bowl and slowly pour over the fat to
cover by at least 1 cm/½ inch, making sure that there are no
trapped bubbles of air.

At this point the confit can be covered and chilled for up
to 2 weeks. You can, of course, roast it straight away.

To serve, preheat the oven to 200°C/400°F/gas mark 6.

If it has been chilled, allow the pork to return to room
temperature. Scoop out 2–4 tablespoons of the pork fat, and
put in a roasting tray. Add the apples and pork and roast for
30 minutes or until cooked and crisp.

Slice the confit and serve immediately with some steamed
green vegetables.

Roast Ham

Preparation time: 2 hours, plus cooling time
Serves 4–6

1.4 kg/2 lb 13 oz gammon, boned and rolled
4 large carrots, peeled and roughly sliced
1 onion, peeled and halved
6 large shallots, peeled
1 bay leaf
6–10 cloves
1 litre/1¾ pints organic cider
6–10 tablespoons maple syrup
2 tablespoons grainy mustard
2–3 tablespoons cider

Place the gammon in a large saucepan and add the
vegetables, bay leaf and cloves. Pour in the cider and, if
necessary, top up with water to cover the meat. Set over a
low heat and bring slowly to the boil. Skim off any scum,
and simmer gently for 40 minutes. Remove from the heat
and leave to cool.

Preheat the oven to 200°C/400°F/gas mark 6. Combine
the maple syrup, mustard and cider in a small bowl.
Carefully cut the meat rind off the fat without cutting the
string and score the fat in a criss-cross pattern.

Lay a double thickness of greaseproof paper in a roasting
tin, making sure it comes up over the sides of the tin.
Place the gammon on the top sheet and liberally cover with
the honey mixture. Wrap the sticky meat in the paper and
then wrap in 1 larger sheet. Place in the oven and bake for
20–30 minutes before opening up the parcel, then bake
uncovered for 30 minutes, basting with the juices. Serve hot,
warm or cold.

Pork Hot-Pot

Preparation time: 2 hours 15 minutes
Serves 4–6

4 tablespoons plain flour
freshly ground black pepper and sea salt
600 g/1¼ lb pork fillet, cubed
3 tablespoons olive oil
250 g/8 oz cooking apples (such as Egremont Russet),
    peeled, cored and thinly sliced
2 onions, peeled, halved and sliced
6 ripe plum tomatoes, skinned and sliced
350 ml/12 fl oz fresh chicken or vegetable stock
425 g/14 oz potatoes, peeled and sliced (3mm/⅛ in thick)
50 g/2 oz unsalted butter, melted

Preheat the oven to 180°C/350°F/gas mark 4.

Season the flour with some salt and pepper and lightly
dust the pork in it. Heat 2 tablespoons of the olive oil in a
large non-stick frying pan set over a medium heat. Add the
meat in batches and fry on all side until golden. Place in a
ovenproof dish.

Add the remaining oil to the pan and fry the apples and
onions for 4–5 minutes, or until they become soft and turn
light brown. Tip the cooked apples and onions into the
ovenproof dish. Add the tomatoes, pour in the stock and
season well with salt and freshly ground black pepper.

Place the sliced potatoes on top and brush them with
melted butter. Season again and place in the preheated oven
for 1–1½ hours, or until the meat is tender. A skewer pushed
through the potatoes into the pork should meet with no
resistance. (If the potatoes begin to get too brown, cover
them with foil.) Serve with green vegetables.

Mushroom and Calvados Risotto

Preparation time: 1 hour
Serves 4

50 g/2 oz unsalted butter
250 g/8 oz mixed wild mushrooms, cleaned
25 g/1 oz dried porcini mushrooms
2 tablespoons olive oil
1 onion, peeled and chopped
1 garlic clove, peeled and crushed
1 bay leaf
450 g/14½ oz risotto rice
6 tablespoons Calvados
750 ml/1¼ pints vegetable stock
freshly ground black pepper and sea salt
100 g/3½ oz fresh Parmesan cheese, finely grated,
    plus extra to serve
small bunch of fresh flat-leaf parsley, chopped

Melt the butter in a frying pan over a medium heat, add the
wild mushrooms and fry until tender. Set aside and keep
warm until needed.

Put the porcini mushrooms in a jug and cover with boiling
water. Leave until tender, then drain them (reserving the
liquid) and chop finely.

Heat the oil in a frying pan, add the onion and garlic and
fry for 6 minutes, then add the bay leaf. Stir in the rice and
continue to fry for a further 3 minutes, stirring regularly.
Add the Calvados and reserved mushroom liquid and cook
until the liquid has nearly evaporated. Slowly add the stock,
stirring well between each addition. Lower the heat and cook
until the rice is al dente, stirring occasionally. Add all the
mushrooms, season and warm through. Stir in the grated
Parmesan and parsley.

Serve with extra Parmesan.

Baked Sea Bass with a Creamy Horseradish Sauce

Preparation time: 55 minutes
Serve 4–6

sauce
100 g/3½ oz creamed horseradish
100 ml/3½ fl oz double cream, lightly whipped
zest of 1 lemon
1 apple (such as Granny Smith), peeled and grated
2 tablespoons fresh dill, finely chopped
freshly ground black pepper

sea bass
1 x 1.4 kg/3 lb sea bass, gutted and de-scaled
handful of fresh mixed herbs, such as chervil, dill parsley
1 lime, thinly sliced
drizzle of good olive oil

Preheat the oven to 220°C/425°F/gas mark 7.

To make the sauce, mix together all the ingredients and season to taste. Cover and set aside until needed.

Line a roasting tray with foil, then greaseproof paper. Place the fish on top and tuck the herbs and half the lime slices into the cavity of the fish. Season the skin of the fish well and drizzle with the oil. Place the remaining lime over the fish. Fold the greaseproof and foil over the fish making a 'tent', seal the edges firmly by twisting them together, and bake for 35 minutes, or until the thickest part of the fish flakes easily when tested with a knife.

Carefully remove the cooked bass from the tray and place on a board. To serve, open the 'tent', remove the flesh from the bone, turn the fish over and do the same on the other side. Place on to warm plates and serve with the sauce.

Skate Wings with Apple and Pineapple Salsa

Preparation time: 50 minutes
Serves 6

salsa
1 small ripe pineapple, peeled, cored and diced
1 red apple (such as Braeburn), cored and diced
1 ripe avocado, peeled and diced
3 spring onions, trimmed and sliced
1 red chilli, deseeded and finely chopped
small bunch of fresh chervil, roughly chopped, plus extra to garnish
small bunch of fresh flat-leaf parsley, roughly chopped, plus extra to garnish
100 ml/3 fl oz extra virgin olive oil
juice of 1 lemon

skate
100 g/3½ oz ghee or clarified butter (see page 11)
juice of 2 lemons
juice of 1 orange
6 x 400 g/13 oz skate wings
freshly ground black pepper and sea salt

Preheat the oven to 180°C/350°F/gas mark 4.

To make the salsa, put all the ingredients except the oil and lemon juice in a bowl, then pour over the oil and lemon juice and season. Mix well, cover and set aside until needed.

Divide the ghee and the lemon and orange juices between two ovenproof dishes large enough to hold three skate wings each. Put the dishes in the oven to melt the ghee. Season the skate wings with a little salt and pepper. Put the skate wings in the ovenproof dishes and bake in the preheated oven for 20–30 minutes, or until the fish flakes when tested with a knife, and is opaque.

To serve, transfer the skate to warm serving plates. Pour the cooking juices over the fish and top with the salsa. Garnish with chopped chervil and parsley.

Vegetables

Apple and Potato Gratin Dauphinoise

Preparation time: 1 hour 15 minutes
Serves 4–6

600 g/1¼ lb waxy potatoes
400 g/13 oz cooking apples (such as Discovery)
50 g/2 oz unsalted butter, softened, plus extra for greasing
1 large garlic clove, peeled and finely chopped
freshly ground black pepper and sea salt
400 ml/14 fl oz double cream
50 g/2 oz Parmesan cheese, freshly grated
50 g/2 oz mature Cheddar cheese

Preheat the oven to 180°C/350°F/gas mark 4.

Peel and finely slice the potatoes, either with a mandoline or in a food processor. Peel, core and finely slice the apples in the same way. Mash the butter and garlic together and season well with pepper and salt.

Grease a wide, shallow ovenproof dish. Arrange a neat layer of potato slices in the bottom of the dish, then dot them with the garlic butter, arrange a layer of apple slices on top and then pour over a little cream. Repeat these alternate layers until all the ingredients have been used, finishing with a layer of potato. Pour over the remaining cream and sprinkle over the Parmesan and Cheddar cheese.

Put the dish on a baking sheet and bake in the oven for 1 hour, or until the potato is tender and the top is golden.

Red Cabbage with Apple and Cassis

Preparation time: 3 hours 45 minutes
Serves 6

1 large red cabbage
2 tablespoons olive oil
18 shallots, peeled
75 g/3 oz sultanas
300 ml/½ pint fresh vegetable stock
450 g/14½ oz redcurrant jelly
2 cooking apples (such as Bramley), peeled and chopped
    into bite-sized chunks
150 ml/¼ pint crème de cassis
freshly ground black pepper and sea salt
fresh blackcurrants, to garnish

Preheat the oven to 160°C/325°F/gas mark 3.

Remove the tough outer leaves of the cabbage, then cut the cabbage in half and cut away the tough white core. Roughly slice, put in a colander and wash. Heat the oil in a frying pan, then add the shallots and fry over a medium heat for 15 minutes, or until soft and golden brown.

Put the cabbage, shallots and sultanas in a large ovenproof dish. Add the stock and redcurrant jelly. Cover and cook in the oven for 2 hours, stirring from time to time.

If the cabbage has become dry, add a little water, then add the apples and crème de cassis. Stir well and return to the oven for a further hour.

Just before serving, season to taste. Put the cabbage in a warm serving bowl and garnish with blackcurrants.

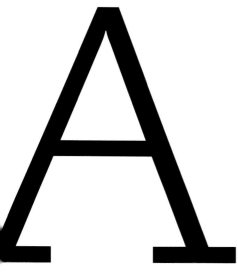lthough they are traditionally associated with desserts, apples are also excellent when combined with vegetables and salads. Their sharp acidity softens when they are cooked, bringing out a slightly sweeter flavour that makes other vegetables taste fresher and lighter. Their texture varies dramatically according to how you prepare them: baked apples have a soft, fluffy consistency; raw apples are fresh and crunchy; and grated apples melt in the mouth. A famously good accompaniment to pork and game, the sweet-acid taste of apples cuts through heavy flavours and cleanses the palate. For salads and light meals, apples provide a juicy burst of freshness that proves they should not be restricted to dessert.

Baked Beetroot and Apple

Preparation time: 55 minutes
Serves 6

6 cooked whole beetroot, peeled
2–4 apples (such as Cox's)
5 tablespoons olive oil
2 tablespoons apple balsamic vinegar
2 tablespoons finely chopped fresh rosemary
1 tablespoon fresh thyme leaves
1 fresh bay leaf, roughly torn
freshly ground black pepper and sea salt

Preheat the oven to 180°C/350°F/gas mark 4.

Cut the beetroot in half and put in a large ovenproof dish. Peel and core the apples, cut them in half and add them to the dish with the beetroot.

Whisk together the oil and vinegar. Add the rosemary, thyme and bay leaf and season to taste with salt and pepper. Pour over the beetroot and apples. Bake in the oven for 40 minutes, or until the apples are soft yet keep their shape.

Serve the baked bettroot and apples while still warm.

Roasted Cumin Apples

Preparation time: 40 minutes
Serves 6

1 kg/2 lb red apples (such as Red Pippin)
50 g/2 oz butter, melted
2 tablespoons honey
1½ teaspoons ground cumin
freshly ground black pepper and sea salt
lightly toasted cumin seeds, to garnish

Preheat the oven to 180°C/350°F/gas mark 4. Core the apples and cut into chunky wedges.

Meanwhile, melt the butter with the honey and ground cumin. Put the apples in a roasting tray, pour over the cumin butter and toss to coat. Season well and roast in the centre of the oven for 20 minutes, turning regularly, until the apples are soft but keep their shape.

To toast the cumin seeds for the garnish, heat a dry heavy frying pan, add several cumin seeds and heat until they begin to smell fragrant.

To serve, transfer the apples to a warm serving bowl and scatter over the cumin seeds.

Wild Rice with Apple and Dried Cranberry Salad

Preparation time: 1 hour, plus 1 hour soaking time
Serves 6

salad
125 g/4 oz wild rice
100 g/3½ oz pecan halves
150 g/5 oz dried cranberries
100 ml/3½ fl oz apple juice, warmed
2 apples (such as Cox's or Russet)
small bunch of chives, roughly chopped
handful of fresh flat-leaf parsley, roughly chopped
1 small red onion, peeled and finely chopped
½ cucumber, finely diced
freshly ground black pepper and sea salt

dressing
1 tablespoon wholegrain mustard
5 tablespoons extra virgin olive oil
1 tablespoon cider vinegar
2 tablespoons apple juice

Bring a large saucepan of salted water to the boil, add the wild rice, stir and return to the boil. Cover and simmer for about 40 minutes, until just tender, or according to the instructions on the packet. Drain well and leave to cool.

Meanwhile, preheat the grill to medium. Spread the pecan halves on a baking sheet and put under the grill, stirring occasionally, until the nuts are lightly and evenly toasted. Leave them to cool.

To make the dressing, put the mustard in a small bowl and slowly whisk in the oil. Stir in the vinegar and apple juice. Season to taste, then set side until needed.

Place the dried cranberries and warm apple juice in a bowl and leave to soak for about 1 hour.

Quarter, core and roughly chop the apples. Put the apples and all the remaining salad ingredients in a bowl and toss thoroughly. Drain the cranberries, reserving the juice. Add the cranberries to the salad and season to taste.

Just before serving, whisk the reserved juice into the dressing, then pour over the salad and toss all the ingredients together so they are evenly combined.

Parsnip, Celery and Grated Apple Rosti

Preparation time: 35 minutes
Serves 3–4

750 g/1½ lb parsnips, peeled
3 apples (such as Russet), peeled and cored
1 celery stick, very finely diced
25 g/1 oz unsalted butter, melted
1 large organic egg, lightly beaten
freshly ground black pepper and sea salt
sunflower oil, for frying

Grate the parsnips and apples into a bowl and squeeze out any excess liquid. Add the celery, butter and egg and season well with salt and pepper.

Heat a little oil in a frying pan over a medium heat. Put a couple of heaped tablespoons of the mixture in the pan and fry for 3–4 minutes, then turn over and fry the second side for a further 3–4 minutes. They will spread out during the cooking process to about 6–7 cm/2½–3 in. Drain on kitchen paper and keep warm until needed. Repeat with the remaining mixture.

Fried Cabbage with Grated Apple and Carrot

Preparation time: 20 minutes
Serves 4–6

1 Savoy cabbage
1 large cooking apple, peeled and cored
1 tablespoon lemon juice
3 carrots, peeled
groundnut oil, for frying
1 tablespoon black mustard seeds
10 fresh curry leaves

Cut the cabbage into quarters and cut away the hard, white core. Thinly slice the cabbage and put into a large bowl. Finely grate the apple into the bowl and toss in the lemon juice. Then finely grate in the carrots.

Heat the oil in a wok or large frying pan over a medium heat. Add the mustard seeds and curry leaves, then fry for 2–3 minutes, or until the seeds start to pop. Add the cabbage, apple and carrots, and stir-fry for 5 minutes, or until the cabbage is tender.

Swiss Chard, Apple and Pine Nuts

Preparation time: 50 minutes
Serves 6

750 g/1½ lb Swiss chard
3–4 apples (such as Laxton)
50 g/2 oz unsalted butter
freshly ground black pepper and sea salt
150 g/5 oz pine nuts, lightly toasted

Trim the Swiss chard and discard any leaves that don't look too good. Slice the leaves and the white stalks, put in a colander and wash. Peel, core and roughly chop the apples. Melt the butter in a frying pan, add the apples and fry for 5–6 minutes, or until soft.

Meanwhile, bring a saucepan of salted water to the boil, then add the chard. Cover and cook for 2–4 minutes, or until the chard is tender. Drain thoroughly, season well with salt and pepper and toss in the pine nuts. Add the fried apple to the chard and mix together.

Serve in a warm serving bowl.

Apple and Celeriac Mash

Preparation time: 40 minutes
Serves 4–6

1 large celeriac, peeled and roughly chopped
1 fennel head, trimmed and chopped
2 cooking apples (such as Bramley), peeled and
   roughly chopped
150 ml/¼ pint clotted cream
cracked black pepper and sea salt
small handful chopped fennel fronds, to garnish
olive oil, to serve

Bring a saucepan of salted water to the boil. Add the celeriac and fennel and boil for 8–10 minutes. Add the apples to the pan, cover and cook for a further 6–8 minutes or until they are tender. Drain, return the vegetables and apple to the saucepan and set over a low heat until all the moisture has evaporated.

Put the vegetable mixture in a food blender and whizz until smooth. Transfer to a bowl, stir in the cream and season with salt and freshly ground black pepper to taste.

Serve in a warm serving bowl and garnish with fennel fronds, cracked black pepper and drizzled with some good quality olive oil.

Puddings

Apple and Cardamom Tarte Tatin

Preparation time: 1 hour 15 minutes
Serve 6

225 g/7½ oz plain flour
50 g/2 oz icing sugar
1 large organic egg
few drops of vanilla extract
300 g/10 oz unsalted butter
200 g/7 oz caster sugar
1 kg/2 lb apples (such as Cox's)
juice of 1 lemon

Preheat the oven to 220°C/425°F/gas mark 7.

Place the flour, icing sugar, egg, vanilla extract and half the butter in the bowl of a food processor and quickly whizz until the mixture looks like coarse crumbs. On a clean work surface, knead lightly until the mixture forms a smooth dough. Wrap in clingfilm and chill for 20 minutes.

Melt the remaining butter in a 20 cm/8 in ovenproof frying pan, add the caster sugar and remove from the heat. Peel, quarter and core the apples, reserving one apple half for the centre of the tart. Place this apple half in the middle the frying pan and tightly pack the apple quarters around it. Cook the apples over a gentle heat for about 15 minutes, or until they are well caramelised all over. Add the lemon juice and remove the pan from the heat. (This method also works well if the ingredients are split between two small frying pans).

On a lightly floured work surface roll out the pastry to fit the frying pan. Place it over the apples and slide the frying pan into the oven. Bake the tart for 25 minutes, or until the pastry is golden.

Remove the pan from the oven and leave for 5 minutes to allow the tart to cool slightly. Invert the tart onto a warm plate and serve.

Calvados and Vanilla Ice Cream

Preparation time: 20 minutes, plus 1 hour infusing time and overnight freezing time
Serves 6–8

600 ml/1 pint double cream
300 ml/½ pint full-fat milk
2 long organic vanilla pods, split
6 large organic egg yolks
50 g/2 oz caster sugar
3–4 tablespoons Calvados

Heat the cream, milk and vanilla pods in a heavy-based saucepan to just below boiling point. Remove from the heat and leave to infuse for about 1 hour. Remove the pods and scrape as many of the seeds as you can back into the cream.

Meanwhile, beat the egg yolks and sugar together in a bowl until a ribbon is left on the surface. Pour over the cream mixture, whisking it in as you pour. Return the custard to the pan and heat very gently, stirring until it thickens enough to lightly coat the back of a wooden spoon. Pour into a clean bowl and leave to cool, then add the Calvados and mix well.

Pour the mixture into a freezer container, cover and put in the freezer. Remove every few hours and gently whisk, then return to the freezer. Repeat until the ice cream is frozen; this will ensure that the ice cream has an even texture.

Put a large baking sheet in the freezer for about 30 minutes. Remove the ice cream and scoop it into large balls, then arrange on the chilled baking sheet. (The ice cream will be soft because of the Calvados.) Return to the freezer.

A few minutes before serving, remove the ice cream from the freezer and place the scoops in chilled bowls.

Apple Charlotte

Preparation time: 55 minutes
Serves 6

butter, for greasing
4 cooking apples (such as Bramley)
75 g/3 oz unsalted butter
250 g/8 oz light brown sugar
1½ tablespoons ground cinnamon
10 thin slices of bread from a large organic traditional
  white loaf
100 g/3½ oz ghee or clarified butter, melted (see page 11)
25 g/1 oz caster sugar

to serve
285 ml/9 fl oz double cream
4 tablespoons Calvados
icing sugar, to taste

Preheat the oven to 180°C/350°F/gas mark 4. Grease a
1.2 litre ml/2 pint oval ovenproof dish.

Peel, core and finely slice the apples. Put in a saucepan
with the butter, sugar and 1 tablespoon of the cinnamon.
Cook gently until the apples have broken up and formed a
purée, then increase the heat to evaporate the excess liquid,
stirring all the time to prevent the purée from burning. Pour
the mixture into the dish.

Cut off the crusts from the bread slices and cut the slices
in half diagonally. Dip each triangle into the melted ghee and
arrange on top of the apple. Sprinkle with sugar and the
remaining cinnamon. Bake in the oven for 30 minutes, or
until the top is golden and crunchy.

To serve, lightly whip the double cream with the Calvados
and sweeten to taste with icing sugar.

Serve the pudding hot or warm with the cream.

Apple Clafoutis

Preparation time: 45 minutes, plus 1 hour
standing time
Serves 4–6

butter, for greasing
50 g/2 oz plain flour
75 g/3 oz caster sugar
3 large organic eggs, plus 1 yolk
seeds from 1 vanilla pod
200 ml/7 fl oz whole milk
450 g/14½ oz apples (such as Fuji), peeled, cored
  and thinly sliced
icing sugar, to decorate

to serve
285 ml/9 fl oz double cream, to serve
2 tablespoons golden syrup, to serve

Preheat the oven to 200°C/400°F/gas mark 6. Grease an
800 ml/1¼ pint ovenproof dish.

Put the flour, sugar, eggs, egg yolk, vanilla seeds and milk
in a food processor and whizz until they form a smooth
batter. Pour into a jug and leave to rest for 1 hour.

Arrange the apple slices, overlapping, in the bottom of
the dish and pour over the batter. If the apples float up,
gently press them back into the batter. Bake in the oven for
25 minutes, or until set and golden on top.

Meanwhile, whip the double cream and golden syrup into
soft peaks, then cover and set aside until needed.

To serve, dust the clafoutis with icing sugar, cut into slices
and accompany with the golden syrup cream.

Apple and Star Anise Strudel

Preparation time: 55 minutes, plus 2–3 hours
soaking time
Serves 6

butter, for greasing
50 ml/2 fl oz Calvados
175 g/6 oz sultanas
150 g/5 oz dark muscovado sugar, plus extra
    for sprinkling
3 star anise, crushed to a powder
juice of 1 lemon
3–4 apples (such as Braeburn)
8 sheets of filo pastry
50 g/2 oz butter, melted
double cream, to serve

Preheat the oven to 190°C/375°F/gas mark 5 and lightly grease a baking sheet.

Pour the Calvados into a saucepan, bring up to the boil then remove from the heat. Add the sultanas and set aside for 2–3 hours.

Mix together the sugar, star anise, lemon juice and Calvados-soaked sultanas. Peel, quarter and core the apples, then chop into smallish chunks and add to the sultana mixture and mix in well.

Lay 2 sheets of filo on the baking sheet, slightly overlapping to make a rectangle about 35 cm/14 in long. Brush with melted butter, then place 2 more sheets on top and brush with butter. Repeat twice more. Spoon the apple mixture evenly over the filo, leaving a border of 3–4 cm/1¼–1½ in around the edge. Fold the side edges over the apple and brush with butter. Slowly and carefully roll up the filo – the folded side edges should seal the ends of the roll. Once rolled, turn the ends inwards to make a horseshoe shape. Brush the top with a little melted butter and sprinkle with the remaining sugar. Bake the strudel in the oven for 30–40 minutes, or until the apples are soft and the filo pastry is golden.

To serve, transfer the strudel from the baking tray on to a warm serving plate. Serve hot or warm with double cream.

Baked Apple Puff

Preparation time: 1 hour 10 minutes
Serves 6

unsalted butter, for greasing
75 g/3 oz pecans, lightly toasted and roughly chopped
1 long vanilla pod
50 g/2 oz light brown sugar
50 g/2 oz unsalted butter, softened
6 apples (such as Braeburn)
30 g/1½ oz white marzipan
150 g/5 oz fresh puff pastry
1 organic egg, beaten
maple syrup, to serve

Preheat the oven to 190°C/375°F/gas mark 5. Grease six
125 ml/4 fl oz ramekins and put them in the fridge to chill.

Put the nuts in a small bowl. Using the tip of a knife,
scrape the seeds out of the vanilla pod then add them to the
nuts along with the sugar and butter, mixing well. Cut the
vanilla pod into six equal lengths and set aside.

Using an apple corer, remove the core from each apple.
Divide the marzipan into six and roll into balls. Push
a marzipan ball into one end of each apple, so it acts as a
stopper (you may have to mould it to fit). Push a bit of
vanilla pod into the marzipan, so it looks like a stem, then
tightly pack the hole with the nut butter. Put each apple into
a ramekin, marzipan down.

Lightly flour the work surface and roll out the pastry.
Cut out six 8–10 cm/3–4 in circles. Lightly brush one side of
each circle with beaten egg and lay them over the apples.
Press the circles on to the ramekins and brush with beaten
egg. Chill for 20 minutes.

Bake the apples in the oven for 25 minutes, or until the
pastry is well risen and golden brown.

To serve, run a knife around the inside of the ramekins to
loosen the apples and invert to turn out. Serve pastry-side
down, drizzled with maple syrup.

Nutmeg Rice Pudding

Preparation time: 1 hour 40 minutes
Serves 6

butter, for greasing
100 g/3½ oz light muscovado sugar, plus extra to serve
1 tablespoon freshly grated nutmeg, plus extra to serve
1–2 tablespoons Calvados
100 g/3½ oz short-grain pudding rice
100 ml/3½ fl oz double cream
600 ml/1 pint full-fat Jersey milk
200 g/7 oz apple purée, warmed

Preheat the oven to 150°C/300°F/gas mark 2. Liberally
grease a 1.5 litre/2½ pint ovenproof dish.

Put the sugar, nutmeg and Calvados in the dish and mix
together before stirring in the rice, cream and milk. Cover
the dish tightly with a piece of greased foil, place on a baking
sheet and bake in the oven for 1½ hours, stirring from time
to time, or until the rice is very tender and the liquid has
been absorbed.

Transfer the hot rice pudding to a warmed serving bowl
and ripple the apple purée through the pudding. Sprinkle
with extra sugar and a little grated nutmeg. It also tastes
when served cold.

Open Apple Pie

Preparation time: 1 hour
Serves 4–6

250 g/8 oz sweet shortcrust pastry
750 g/1½ lb small sweet apples (such as Cox's,
    Worcester or Discovery)
juice of 1 lemon
175 g/6 oz light soft brown sugar
1½ teaspoons freshly grated nutmeg
1½ teaspoons ground cinnamon
50 g/2 oz unsalted butter, chilled and cubed
1 tablespoon caster sugar
2 tablespoons milk, heated
runny honey, for drizzling
ice cream, to serve

Preheat the oven to 200°C/400°F/gas mark 6.

Lightly flour the worksurface and roll out the pastry
to fit a 20 cm/8 in springform cake tin (about 6–8 cm/
2½–3½ in deep). Line the tin with the pastry and chill
until needed.

Peel, quarter and core the apples. Slice the quarters into
four and toss the slices in the lemon juice. Put the brown
sugar, nutmeg and cinnamon into a bowl, mix, then add the
apples and stir to coat them with the sugar. Put the apple
mixture in the pastry case and dot with the butter. Dissolve
the caster sugar in the hot milk and brush the mixture over
the pastry edges.

Bake the pie in the oven for 40 minutes, or until the
apples are golden and soft. Remove the pie from the tin and
serve hot or warm, drizzled with honey and accompanied
with a scoop of ice cream.

Pink Lady Apple Fritters

Preparation time: 40 minutes, plus 1 hour
standing time
Serves 6

6 firm Pink Lady apples
juice of 1 lemon
200 g/7 oz self-raising flour, sifted
300 ml/½ pint soda water
sunflower oil, for deep-frying
caster sugar, to decorate
ice cream, to serve

Peel and core the apples and chop into rings or chunks.
Squeeze over some lemon juice to prevent them from going
brown. Put the flour in a food processor and switch on.
Slowly add the soda water, whizzing until it forms a thickish
batter, similar to Yorkshire pudding batter. Pour into a jug
and leave to rest for 1 hour.

Heat the oil in a deep-fat fryer to 180°C/350°F, or until
a cube of bread browns in 1 minute. Pat dry the apple
rings/chunks on kitchen paper. Pour the batter into a large
bowl. Put all the apple into the batter and once fully coated
drop a few pieces at a time into the hot oil. Cook for about
4 minutes until crisp and golden, then remove and drain on
kitchen paper. Sprinkle liberally with caster sugar. Repeat
until all the apples have been fried. Put the fritters in a warm
oven while you fry the reminder.

Serve the fritters warm with a scoop of vanilla ice cream.

Apple and Blackberry Alpen Crumble

Preparation time: 50 minutes
Serves 6

butter, for greasing
3–4 cooking apples (such as Bramley)
250 g/8 oz blackberries
175 g/6 oz caster sugar
zest of 1 orange
50 ml/2 fl oz orange liqueur
100 g/3½ oz plain flour
100 g/3½ oz unsalted butter, chilled
200 g/7 oz original Alpen
custard, to serve

Preheat the oven to 180°C/350°F/gas mark 4. Grease a 800 ml–1 litre/1¼–1¾ pint oval ovenproof dish.

Peel, core and roughly chop the apples, and put them in a bowl. Add the blackberries, 100 g/3½ oz of the sugar and the orange zest and liqueur and mix well. Spoon into the prepared ovenproof dish.

Sift the flour into a bowl and add the remaining sugar. Roughly chop the butter and, using your fingertips, rub it in until the mixture resembles breadcrumbs. Add the Alpen and mix well, then spoon the crumble mixture over the fruit.

Bake in the oven for 25 minutes, or until the crumble is hot in the centre and golden on top.

Serve hot or warm with custard.

Apple Snow

Preparation time: 20 minutes
Serves 4

2 cooking apples, peeled, cored and roughly chopped
juice of 1 lemon
zest of 1 orange
50–75 g/2–3 oz caster sugar, to taste
3 large organic egg whites
thin strips of orange zest, to decorate

Place the chopped apples in a pan with the lemon juice and about 75–100 ml of water. Cover with a lid and cook for about 10 minutes, or until the apples have become a purée. Remove the pan from the heat and leave to cool.

Once the apple purée has cooled stir in the caster sugar and orange zest.

In a clean bowl whisk the egg whites until they form soft peaks. The tips of the beaten whites should gently fall over when you remove the whisk. Don't overwhisk or the apple snow will be rather flat. Using a metal spoon gently fold the apple mixture into the beaten egg whites taking care not to flatten all the air you have carefully beaten in. Chill the mixture until needed.

To serve, spoon the mixture into 4 glasses and decorate with thin strips of orange zest.

Appleade and Elderflower Jelly

Preparation time: 15 minutes, plus standing and
chilling time
Serves 6

25 g/1 oz gelatine powder
100 ml/3½ fl oz elderflower cordial
800 ml/1¼ pints appleade
elderflowers, to decorate if available

Pour 2 tablespoons of cold water into a small bowl and
sprinkle over the gelatine powder. Leave for 5–6 minutes,
or until the gelatine is springy.

Put the bowl over a saucepan of hot water and let the
gelatine completely dissolve over a medium heat – do not let
it get too hot. Pour the dissolved gelatine into the elderflower
cordial and leave for 30 minutes. Add the appleade and pour
the mixture into six 125 ml/4 fl oz moulds or glasses. Chill
overnight, or until the jelly has become firm.

To serve, dip the moulds in hot water for just a few
seconds. Cover each mould with a cold plate and, holding
the mould and plate firmly together, give them a sharp shake
to turn out. Decorate with elderflowers if available and serve.

Poached Apples and Mangoes in Rosewater

Preparation time: 45 minutes
Serves 4

100 g/3½ oz caster sugar
2 tablespoons rosewater
200 ml/7 fl oz dessert wine (such as Sauternes)
1 lemon
4 apples (such as Worcester)
100 g/3½ oz semi-dried mango slices
crème fraîche, to serve
undyed rose petals, to decorate

Put the sugar, rosewater and wine in a saucepan with about
300 ml/½ pint water. Using a potato peeler, remove strips of
peel from the lemon and add them to the pan. Set the
saucepan over a medium heat and stir occasionally, letting
the sugar dissolve. Peel, halve and core the apples. Squeeze
over some lemon juice to prevent them from going brown.
Add the apples to the saucepan, making sure that they are
covered (you may need to add a little more water). Cook for
15 minutes, then add the mango slices and cook for a further
10 minutes, or until the apples are soft but still hold their
shape. Leave until cold.

Serve in a chilled glass bowl with some crème fraîche and
scatter with rose petals to decorate.

Apple and Dried Fruits Christmas Pudding

Preparation time: 50 minutes
Serves 8

250 g/8 oz sultanas
250 g/8 oz raisins
200 g/7 oz dates, roughly chopped
200 g/7 oz figs, roughly chopped
150 g/5 oz dried apricots, roughly chopped
150 g/5 oz dried apples, roughly chopped
200 ml/7 fl oz brandy, warmed, plus exra to serve
zest of 1 orange
zest of 1 lemon
200 g/7 oz white breadcrumbs
200 g/7 oz mixture of hazelnuts and almonds, lightly
    toasted and chopped
75 g/3 oz plain flour
1 teaspoon ground mixed spice
200 g/7 oz shredded suet
225 g/7½ oz soft brown sugar
100 g/3½ oz treacle
4 large organic eggs, lightly beaten

Place the sultanas, raisins, dates, figs, dried apricots and dried apples in a bowl, pour the brandy over the fruit and leave overnight to soak.

Lightly grease a 1.6 litre/2¾ pint pudding basin and line the base with greaseproof paper.

Place the orange and lemon zest, breadcrumbs, nuts, flour, mixed spice and suet in a large bowl and mix well.

In another bowl whisk together the sugar, treacle and eggs until evenly mixed. Stir in the brandy-soaked fruit, then fold the evenly into the flour and nuts.

Spoon the mixture into the pudding basin, pressing down well. Take a greased sheet of greaseproof paper and fold a simple 2½ cm/1 in pleat across the center. Do the same with a sheet of foil. Cover the pudding with the greaseproof paper and then the foil, securing them tightly under the rim of the pudding basin with string.

Place the pudding in a saucepan large enough to fit the basin and fill the pan with boiling water. Cover and simmer for about 5–6 hours, or until the pudding is firm. When you insert a skewer into the centre, it should come out clean. Remember to check the water level from time to time and top up with boiling water as necessary.

Lift the pudding from the saucepan and leave to cool. The pudding can be stored in an airtight container in a cool dark place for up to 8 weeks.

To serve, steam the pudding, as above, for about 2 hours. Turn out onto a warm plate, pour over some hot brandy and set light to the pudding.

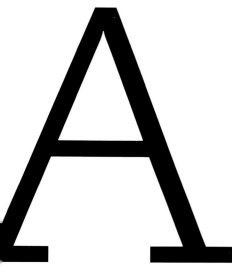pples are the most versatile and fuss-free of fruit – to eat as a snack at any time of the day or to cook with. There are more than seven thousand varieties of apple, though far fewer are seriously marketed. When choosing apples for your kitchen, avoid those with obvious bruises or soft spots, but don't be put off by a few dull, rough, brown patches on sound apples. This is known as russeting and in the case of apples that go by the name of russets, this rough surface can extend over the entire skin. Apples continue to ripen once they have been picked. If you intend to store them for any length of time, spread them out so that they do not touch each other and keep them in a cool, dark, dry place until you need them.

Apple and Toffee Steamed Pudding

Preparation time: 3–3½ hours
Serves 6

butter, for greasing
200 ml/7 fl oz apple purée
2 tablespoons ginger syrup
175 g/6 oz unsalted butter
175 g/6 oz caster sugar
3 large eggs, lightly beaten
a few drops of vanilla flavouring
100 ml/3½ fl oz banoffee toffee sauce
2–4 pieces of stem ginger
175 g/6 oz self-raising flour, sifted

Grease a 1.2 litre/2 pint pudding basin. Spoon the apple purée and ginger syrup evenly into the basin, cover and set aside until needed.

Cream together the butter and sugar until pale and fluffy. Slowly add the beaten eggs, beating well after each addition, then mix in the vanilla and toffee sauce. Pat the pieces of ginger dry and chop into small bits. Toss the ginger into the flour and, using a metal spoon, fold half the flour into the beaten mixture and then add the rest. Spoon the mixture into the basin and cover with a greased, pleated sheet of greaseproof paper, then a pleated layer of foil, and secure tightly under the rim of the basin with string.

Fill a large, deep saucepan with water, cover and heat until it is almost boiling. Stand the basin in a steaming basket and put the basket over the water, cover and cook – with the water always just below boiling point – for 2½–3 hours, or until the pudding is firm. When you insert a skewer into the centre of the pudding it should come out clean. Remember to check the water level in the saucepan from time to time and top up with boiling water as necessary.

To serve, invert the pudding on to a warm plate.

Apple and Lemon Granita

Preparation time: 20 minutes, plus 8–10 hours freezing time
Serves 6

400 ml/14 fl oz clear apple juice
300 ml/½ pint water
200 g/7 oz granulated sugar
juice of 5 large lemons
4–5 tablespoons Calvados (optional)
strips of lemon zest, to decorate

Put the apple juice, water and sugar in a small saucepan. Set over a high heat and stir occasionally until the sugar has dissolved. Remove the syrup from the heat and leave to cool.

Meanwhile, put the lemon juice and Calvados (if using) in a freezer container. Cover and chill.

Once the syrup is cold, pour into the lemon juice and Calvados mixture and put in the freezer. After 2–3 hours remove and, using a fork, mix any ice crystals into the liquid. Return to the freezer and repeat every hour until the slushy mixture forms crystalline ice flakes.

To serve, spoon into shot glasses or small bowls and decorate with strips of lemon zest.

Tea Time Treats

HAS T...
REQUIR
MANN

opped

f horizontally,

s

C/Gas 6. Heat the
e heavy-based pan
to foam. Stir in the
ook for 2 minutes

seeds until brown
a pestle and mortar
. Mix in the curry
ger, then stir into

ple and honey an
. Pour in the sto
duce the heat t

GUY FAWKES

I love Bonfire Night, perhaps because it's one of the few occasions when it is OK to indulge our child-like fascination with fire – from barbecues to bonfires to magnificent fireworks. The food has to be the kind of comforting, unfussy nosh that requires no garnishes or table manners. So I'm offering up three recipes for a very casual gathering.

FOR THE GARLIC BR
2 large garlic cloves, f
1 tbsp chopped parsle
100g butter, softened
1 ciabatta loaf, sliced
  then cut into thick s

1 Heat the oven to 2O
butter and oil in a lar
until the butter begin
onions and garlic and
to soften.
2 Dry-toast the cumi
and fragrant. Grind in
with a pinch of sea sa
powder and ground gi
the onions.
3 Add the parsnips, ap
cook for a few minutes
bring to a boil, then re
simmer for 2O minutes

Toffee Apples

Preparation time: 50 minutes
Makes 18

18 small apples (such as Royal Gala)
18 wooden lollipop sticks
1.4 kg/2 lb 13 oz caster sugar
10 g/⅓ oz lard
3 tablespoons malt vinegar
3 drops cochineal food colouring
cellophane and ribbon, to decorate (optional)

Wipe the apples clean, removing any grease from the skins.
Remove the stalks, insert the wooden sticks and place the
apples on a sheet of greaseproof paper.

Put the remaining ingredients in a saucepan and add
450 ml/¾ pint water. Bring slowly to the boil, then continue
to boil until a sugar thermometer reads 140°C/295°F, the
'cracking' stage. Dip the bottom of the pan in cold water to
stop further cooking. To test without a sugar thermometer,
drop a little of the syrup into very cold water. If it becomes
hard and brittle, the correct temperature has been reached.
Carefully remove from the heat and leave the syrup to cool
slightly for 5–10 minutes.

Dip the apples in the toffee, making sure that each apple
is well covered, then stand them on the greaseproof paper.
Leave to cool and harden.

Wrap in cellophane and tie with ribbon, if wished.

Apple and Pear Scones

Preparation time: 30–35 minutes
Makes 8

450 g/14½ oz plain white flour
pinch of salt
1½ teaspoons baking powder
75 g/3 oz butter, cubed
25 g/1 oz caster sugar
50 g/2 oz each of dried apple and dried pear
1 large organic egg, plus 1 yolk
200 ml/7 fl oz milk
thick double cream and jam, to serve

glaze
1 large organic egg, lightly beaten
2 tablespoons milk

Preheat the oven to 220°C/425°F/gas mark 7.

Sieve the flour, salt and baking powder into a bowl.
Add the butter and rub in, using your fingertips, until the
mixture resembles breadcrumbs. Stir in the sugar and dried
fruits, then make a well in the centre.

Whisk the egg and egg yolk with the milk, add to the
dry ingredients and mix to a soft dough. Turn out on to a
floured board. Lightly shape the dough into a round, flatten
it to a thickness of 3 cm/1 inch and, using a round 6–7 cm/
2½–3 inch cutter, cut out 8 rounds. Arrange the rounds,
spaced evenly apart, on a lightly greased baking sheet.

To make the glaze, lightly beat the egg and milk together.
Brush the rounds with the egg glaze. Bake in the oven for
10–15 minutes until risen and golden-brown. Transfer to
a wire rack and leave to cool.

To serve, break the scones in half and fill with thick
double cream and jam.

Apple Doughnuts

Preparation time: 1 hour, plus proving time
Makes 10–12

1 tablespoon caster sugar
50 ml/2 fl oz warm milk
200 g/7 oz plain flour, plus extra for dusting
7 g/¼ oz quick-action yeast
pinch of salt
50 g/2 oz unsalted butter, softened
1 large organic egg
50 ml/2 fl oz warm water
100 g/3½ oz apple purée
oil, for deep-fat frying
caster sugar and ground cinnamon, to coat

Dissolve the sugar in the milk. Sieve the flour into a bowl, add the yeast and salt and rub in the butter. Lightly beat the egg with the warm water and milk, then pour them into the flour mixture. Lightly fold together, then turn out on to a lightly floured worksurface and knead until smooth.

Transfer the dough to a lightly oiled bowl, cover and leave in a warm place to double in size.

Knock the dough back, knead for 3–5 minutes, then divide into 10–12 pieces. Shape the pieces into rounds, gently roll each round flat and spoon 1–2 teaspoons of apple purée into the centre. Draw the edges together, pinching them well to seal, then reshape to form balls. Spread out the balls on a greased baking tray and leave to prove for about 30 minutes.

Heat the oil in a deep-fat fryer to 180°C/350°F, or until a cube of bread browns in 1 minute. Add 2–3 balls to the fryer and fry for 2–3 minutes until puffed up, golden brown and cooked. Drain on kitchen paper. Repeat with the remaining balls

Toss each doughnut in the sugar-cinnamon coating and serve the same day.

Apple, Carrot and Coconut Muffins with Walnut and Brown Sugar Topping

Preparation time: 50 minutes
Makes 12

12 paper muffin cases
3 large organic eggs, lightly beaten
300 g/10 oz light soft brown sugar
250 ml/8 fl oz sunflower oil
450 g/14½ oz self-raising flour
2 teaspoons ground cinnamon
pinch of salt
300 g/10 oz carrots, coarsely grated
300 g/10 oz apples, peeled and coarsely grated
150 g/5 oz flaked coconut
100 g/3½ oz walnuts, lightly toasted and chopped
2 teaspoons bicarbonate of soda

topping
50 g/2 oz walnuts, lightly toasted and chopped
50 g/2 oz flaked coconut
75 g/3 oz brown sugar

Preheat the oven to 180°C/350°F/gas mark 4. Line a 12-cup muffin tray with muffin cases.

To make the topping, mix together the nuts and sugar in a bowl, then set aside until needed.

Combine the eggs with the sugar and oil in a bowl. Mix together the remaining ingredients in a separate bowl, then fold into the oil mixture. Spoon into the muffin cases and top with the sugary nuts. Bake for 30 minutes, or until well risen and firm to the touch. Spread out on a wire rack and leave to cool. They are best served the same day.

Apples Covered with Chocolate and Nuts

Preparation time: 20 minutes
Serves 4

150 g/5 oz dark or milk chocolate
4 green apples (such as Golden Delicious)
4 wooden sticks
50 g/2 oz hazelnuts, finely chopped and lightly toasted
50 g/2 oz Hundreds & Thousands

Put the chocolate in a bowl and place over a saucepan of boiling water. Make sure that the water does not touch the bottom of the bowl. Keep the water boiling until the chocolate is melted. Remove the chocolate from the heat and leave to cool for about 5 minutes.

Rub the apples with kitchen paper to remove any wax or stickiness. Insert 4 wooden sticks into the apples. Dip or brush the apples with the melted chocolate and place them on a sheet of greaseproof paper. Leave for about 5 minutes, or until nearly set.

Roll 2 apples in the nuts, the other 2 in the Hundreds and Thousands and leave to set completely.

Calvados Fudge

Preparation time: 35 minutes
Makes 36 squares

397 g/13 oz can condensed milk
125 g/4 oz unsalted butter, chopped
450 g/14½ oz caster sugar
2 teaspoons vanilla essence
1 tablespoon Calvados

Grease and line a 20 cm/8 in square baking tin. A Swiss roll tin would be ideal.

Put the condensed milk, butter and sugar in a heavy non-stick saucepan and heat gently, stirring, until the butter and sugar have melted into the milk. Slowly bring to the boil and boil for 10–14 minutes, or until the mixture changes to a golden colour, stirring all the time to prevent it catching on the base of the saucepan.

Remove from the heat, leave to cool for 5 minutes, then stir in the Calvados.

Pour the mixture into the prepared tin and leave to harden before cutting into sqaures.

Apple and Rosemary Cake

Preparation time: 1 hour 20 minutes
Serves 8–10

butter, for greasing
3 small apples (such as Granny Smith), peeled,
    cored and quartered
juice of 1 lemon
200 g/7 oz butter, softened
200 g/7 oz caster sugar
1 teaspoon vanilla extract
4 large organic eggs, lightly beaten
200 g/7 oz self-raising flour

syrup
100 g/3½ oz caster sugar
2 sprigs of rosemary

Preheat the oven to 180°C/350°F/gas mark 4. Grease and
line the bottom of an 22 cm/8½ in springform cake tin.

Toss the apples in the lemon juice and place the apple
quarters in the bottom of the cake tin.

Cream together the butter, sugar and vanilla in a bowl
until light and fluffy. Slowly add the eggs, beating well after
each addition. Fold in the flour.

Spoon the cake mixture into the tin. Bake in the oven for
40–45 minutes or until golden. A skewer inserted in the cake
should come out clean. Leave in the tin and, using a skewer,
prick holes over the top of the cake.

While the cake bakes, make the syrup. Put the sugar in
a pan with 150 ml/1¼ pints water. Dissolve the sugar over
a low heat, add the rosemary then simmer for 15 minutes.
Cover, remove from the heat and leave the syrup to infuse
for 15 minutes.

Pour half the warm syrup over the cake, then repeat in a
couple of hours. Remove from the tin and serve.

Apple and Almond Cake with Butterscotch Sauce

Preparation time: 1 hour 30 minutes
Serves 6–8

butter, for greasing
250 g/8 oz unsalted butter, softened
250 g/8 oz caster sugar
pinch of salt
5 large organic eggs, lightly beaten
75 g/3 oz plain flour
200 g/7 oz ground almonds
2 teaspoons almond essence
2 apples (such as Braeburn), peeled, cored and sliced

sauce
50 g/2 oz unsalted butter
1 tablespoon golden syrup
100 ml/3½ fl oz evaporated milk
125 g/4 oz soft brown sugar

To make the butterscotch sauce, put all the ingredients in a
small saucepan and stir over a low heat until the sugar has
dissolved. Turn up the heat and boil until reduced to a
thick but runny sauce. Set aside and leave to cool.

Preheat the oven to 160°C/325°F/gas mark 3. Grease
a 22 cm/9 in springform cake tin, line the bottom and grease
the lining.

Cream together the butter, sugar and salt in a bowl until
light and fluffy. Slowly add the eggs, beating well after each
addition. Fold in the flour, almonds and almond essence.
Spoon the cake mixture into the tin and place the apples
on top of the mixture. Bake in the oven for about 1¼ hours,
or until golden-brown and firm to the touch. If the cake is
browning too quickly, cover the top with foil and continue
cooking. Leave in the tin for 5 minutes, then turn out on to
a wire rack and leave to cool.

Just before serving, drizzle over the butterscotch sauce,
or serve it in a small jug.

Lemon Poppyseed Cake with Apple Icing

Preparation time: 2 hours
Serves 6–8

butter, for greasing
250 g/8 oz unsalted butter, softened
300 g/10 oz caster sugar
zest of 4 lemons
75 g/3 oz poppy seeds
2 teaspoons vanilla extract
500 g/1 lb plain flour, sifted
1 tablespoon baking powder
300 ml/½ pint milk
5 large organic egg whites
lemon zest, to decorate

icing
4–5 tablespoons clear apple juice
500 g/1 lb icing sugar, sifted

Preheat the oven to 160°C/325°F/gas mark 3.

Grease a 20 cm/8 in springform cake tin, line the bottom and grease the lining.

Cream together the butter and sugar in a bowl until pale. Slowly fold in the lemon zest, poppy seeds, vanilla, flour, baking power and milk to make a soft batter.

Whisk the egg whites in a clean bowl to form soft peaks. Using a large metal spoon, gently fold the egg whites into the mixture. Spoon into the tin and bake in the oven for 1½ hours, or until golden brown and when a skewer is inserted into the centre comes out clean. Leave the cake in the tin for a few minutes, then turn it out on to a wire rack and leave to cool.

To make the icing, put the icing sugar in a bowl and slowly pour in the apple juice, stirring to make a paste; take care not to add too much. Spread over the top of the cake.

Decorate with lemon zest and leave to set.

Pork and Apple Turnovers

Preparation time: 35 minutes
Makes 6

400 g/13 oz ready-to-roll puff pastry
3 good pork sausages, skins removed
1 apple, peeled and grated
1 tablespoon rosemary, very finely chopped
1 tablespoon grainy mustard
freshly ground black pepper and sea salt
1 large organic egg, lightly beaten
25 g/1 oz sesame seeds

Preheat the oven to 180°C/350°F/gas mark 4.

On a lightly floured surface, roll out the puff pastry to a large rectangle. Using a pastry cutter, cut out six 14 cm/ 6 in rounds.

Mix the sausage meat, apple, rosemary and mustard together in a bowl and season well.

Brush the edges of the pastry with the beaten egg. Divide the meat mixture between the six pastry rounds and fold over the pastry to make a parcel. Press the edges tightly together so the filling is sealed in. Brush the outside of each parcel with a little more beaten egg and sprinkle with sesame seeds.

Place on a baking sheet, spaced evenly apart, and bake in the oven for 15–20 minutes or until golden and risen.

Serve either warm or cold.

Apple and Cream Cheese Sandwiches

Preparation time: 15 minutes
Serves 2–4

1 apple (such as Granny Smith)
1 tablespoon lemon juice
350 g/11½ oz cream cheese
1 celery stick, trimmed and finely diced
freshly ground black pepper
8 slices of fresh seed bread (such as soya and linseed)
soft butter, for spreading
handful of cress

Cut the apple into quarters and remove the core. Carefully grate the apple quarters into a bowl, then sprinkle with the lemon juice to prevent them turning brown.

Add the cream cheese and diced celery to the apple and mix well. Season with a little freshly ground black pepper.

Lightly butter the seed bread slices on one side, then spread the cheese mixture over the butter. Lay the apple on four slices of seed bread and sprinkle with cress. Lay the remaining four slices on top and press down lightly.

Remove the crusts, if you wish. Cut the sandwiches into triangles and serve.

Apple Shortbread

Preparation time: 1 hour 30 minutes
Makes 8–10 squares

shortbread
300 g/10 oz butter
100 g/3½ oz caster sugar, plus extra for dusting
350 g/11½ oz plain flour
50 g/2 oz cornflour or ground rice
pinch of salt

apple
2 apples (such as Golden Delicious), peeled, cored
    and thinly sliced
1–2 teaspoons cinnamon powder
50 g/2 oz caster sugar

crumble
250 g/8 oz plain flour
½ teaspoon baking powder
75g/3 oz caster sugar
150 g/5 oz unsalted butter, softened
icing sugar, to decorate

Preheat the oven to 150°C/300°F/gas mark 2.

Grease and line a 20 cm/8 in square tin. To make the
shortbread, cream together the butter and sugar in a bowl.
Sift in the flours and salt and mix well. Press the mixture
into the prepared tin and bake in the oven for 30 minutes.

Put the sliced apples on top of the shortbread, then
sprinkle over the cinnamon and sugar.

Turn the oven up to 190°C/375°F/gas mark 5.

Sift the flour and baking powder into a bowl and add
the sugar. Roughly chop the butter, then rub in, using your
fingertips, until the mixture is crumbly. Spread evenly over
the apple, then bake in the oven for 30 minutes or until the
crumble is golden-brown. Leave to cool in the tin.

Remove the shortbread from the tin and cut into squares.

To decorate, dust with icing sugar.

Apple and Date Sticky Tea Loaf

Preparation time: 1 hour 15 minutes, plus 1 hour
soaking time
Serves 6–8

175 g/6 oz Medjool dates, pitted and roughly chopped
75 g/3 oz semi-dried apples, roughly chopped
100 g/3½ oz unsalted butter
200 g/7 oz caster sugar
2 large organic eggs
1–2 drops vanilla essence
175 g/6 oz plain flour
1 teaspoon baking powder
1 teaspoon bicarbonate of soda
unsalted butter, to serve

Preheat the oven to 170°C/340°F/gas mark 3½. Grease and
line a 10 x 22 cm/4 x 8½ inch loaf tin.

Put the dates and apples in a bowl, pour over 300 ml/
½ pint boiling water and leave to soak for 1 hour.

Cream together the butter and sugar in a bowl until pale
and light. Beat in the eggs, one at a time. Add the vanilla and
fold in the date mixture. Sift the flour, baking powder and
bicarbonate of soda together and fold into the date mixture.
Spoon into the loaf tin and bake in the oven for about
1 hour, or until the loaf has shrunk slightly away from the
sides of the tin and is firm to the touch.

Allow to cool slightly in the tin. Serve while still warm,
cut into slices and lightly spread with unsalted butter.

Apple Pancakes

Preparation time: 30 minutes, plus 30 minutes
standing time
Makes 8

125 g/4 oz plain flour, sieved
pinch of salt
1 large organic egg
300 ml/½ pint milk
a little oil, for frying

to serve
8 heaped tablespoons chocolate spread
150 ml/¼ pint apple purée
icing sugar

Place the flour, salt, egg and milk in a food processor and quickly whizz until the mixture forms a smooth batter. Cover and leave to stand if possible, for at least 30 minutes.

Heat a drop of oil in an 18 cm/7 in heavy-based frying pan. Pour in just enough batter to thinly coat the base of the pan, tipping the pan to help the batter spread. Cook over a medium-high heat for 1 minutes and toss and cook on the other side for about 1½ minutes, or until golden.

Transfer the pancake to a warm plate and keep warm. Repeat with the remaining batter. Stack the pancakes with a layer of greaseproof paper between each one.

To serve, spread a spoonful of chocolate spread over each pancake followed by a spoonful of apple purée. Roll or fold the pancakes and sprinkle with icing sugar.

Apple Tea

Preparation time: 50 minutes
Makes about 2 mugs

4 apples, cored and roughly chopped
1 cinnamon stick
3–5 cloves

Put all the ingredients in a saucepan and cover with cold water. Bring to the boil, then reduce the heat to a simmer. Cover the pan and simmer for 40 minutes.

Pour the tea through a fine sieve and discard the apple, cinnamon and cloves. Pour the hot tea into two warm mugs and serve.

The apple tea can be lightly reheated if necessary.

Side Shows

Cox's Chunky Apple Sauce

Preparation time: 30 minutes
Serves 6

5–6 Cox's apples, peeled, cored and roughly chopped
40 g/1½ oz light brown sugar
125 ml/4 fl oz fresh chicken stock
100 ml/3½ fl oz Calvados
freshly ground black pepper and sea salt

Put the apples, sugar and chicken stock in a large saucepan. Cover and set over a medium heat. Simmer the apples and stock for 10–15 minutes, or until the apples become soft. Using a slotted spoon, remove about one-third of the apples and set them aside. Leave the rest to cool slightly.

Once cool, put the cooked apple mixture in a food processor and whizz until smooth. Alternatively, press it through a sieve using the back of a wooden spoon, or pass it through a mouli legumes. Transfer the apple purée to a bowl and stir in the reserved apple chunks.

Pour the Calvados into a small saucepan, set it over a high heat and boil until the Calvados has reduced to about 50 ml/2 fl oz. Pour the hot Calvados into the apple sauce and season with freshly ground black pepper and sea salt. Serve warm.

Apple and Blackberry Jam

Preparation time: 55 minutes
Makes 5 x 250 g/8 oz jars

1.4 kg/2¾ lb blackberries
450 g/14½ oz cooking apples, peeled, cored and chopped
1.6 kg/3¼ lb jam sugar, warmed
5 jam jars

Preheat the oven to 160°C/325°F/gas mark 3. Wash 5 jam jars in hot, soapy water until entirely clean, then place them on a baking sheet and put in the oven for 10 minutes. Keep warm before the jam is ready.

Wash the blackberries, and put them in a large preserving pan. Add the chopped apple, sugar and 150 ml/¼ pint water, then simmer until the fruit becomes soft. Place over a low heat until the sugar has entirely dissolved, stirring all the time. Bring to the boil over a medium heat, stirring constantly with a wooden spoon. Boil for 20 minutes, skimming the surface with a slotted metal spoon to remove any scum that forms.

Meanwhile, put a saucer in the freezer or fridge for 20 minutes. To test if the jam is done, remove the pan from the heat, spoon a teaspoonful of the jam on to the saucer and leave for 1 minute. Then use your finger and run it through the jam – it should wrinkle up. If not, continue to boil the jam for another 10 minutes and then retest.

Using a small ladle, fill the warm jars with the jam to within 1 cm/½ inch of the top, then wipe them clean. Put a disc of waxed paper wax side down on top of the jam and seal the jars with airtight lids. Leave to cool, then label and store in a cool, dark, dry place.

Apple and Raspberry Jam

Preparation time: 40 minutes, plus 12 hours
soaking time
Makes 6 x 250 g/8 oz jars

6 jam jars
1 kg/2 lb raspberries
1 kg/2 lb jam sugar
500 g/1 lb cooking apples, peeled and cored
6 tablespoons lemon juice

Preheat the oven to 160°C/325°F/gas mark 3.

Put the raspberries in a large non-metal bowl and mix in
the sugar. Cover and leave overnight.

Wash 6 jam jars in hot, soapy water until entirely clean,
then place them on a baking sheet and put in the oven for
10 minutes. Keep warm before the jam is ready.

Preheat the oven to 110°C/225°F/gas mark G. Put the jam
jars on a baking sheet in the oven for 5 minutes, then stand
them on a clean towel, open side down.

Chop the apples into raspberry-sized pieces. Put the
raspberries, apples, sugar and lemon juice in a preserving
pan. Bring to the boil over a medium heat, stirring constantly
with a wooden spoon. Boil for 20 minutes, and use a slotted
spoon to remove any scum that forms on the surface.

Meanwhile, put a saucer in the freezer or fridge for 20
minutes. To test to see if the jam is done, remove the pan
from the heat, spoon a teaspoon of jam on to the saucer and
leave for 1 minute. Then use your fingertip to push the jam
– it should wrinkle up. If not, boil the jam for another
10 minutes and retest.

Using a small ladle, fill the warm, sterilized jars with the
jam to within 1 cm/½ inch of the top, then wipe them clean.
Put a disc of waxed paper on top of the jam wax side down
and seal with airtight lids. Leave to cool, then label and store
in a cool, dark, dry place.

Golden Delicious Dried Apple Rings

Preparation time: 8 hours 15 minutes, plus 10 minutes
steeping time
Makes about 30–35

juice of 2 large lemons
1 kg/2 lb green apples (such as Golden Delicious)
25 g/1 oz caster sugar

Preheat the oven to 140°C/275°F/gas mark 1.

Put the lemon juice in a bowl and half fill with cold water.
Peel and core the apples and slice them into rings. Add the
rings to the bowl, making sure that they are well covered
with the water and juice. The lemon juice will stop the
apples turning brown. Leave for 10 minutes.

Drain the apples, then put the rings on kitchen paper and
pat them dry. Spread out the rings on a large baking tray and
bake them in the preheated oven for 8 hours, turning once or
twice. After about 5 hours, lightly sprinkle the apple slices
with a little caster sugar on one side.

Leave to cool, then store in an airtight container.

Pork Scratchings and Apple Chips

Preparation time: 1 hour 15 minutes
Serves 6–8

500 g/1 lb pork rind, scored into small diamonds
250 g/8 oz sea salt, plus extra to serve
2 red apples (such as Royal Gala or Discovery), cored
oil, for deep-frying

Preheat the oven to 200°C/400°F/gas mark 6.

Heat a large frying pan on the hob until you can feel the heat rising from the pan. Press the rind down on to the hot pan. It will spit like mad, so take care not to burn your hands. Fry for about 5 minutes, or until the rind starts to change colour. Transfer to a roasting tray and sprinkle with 150 g/5 oz sea salt. Roast in the oven for about 30 minutes, or until the crackling is golden and very crispy. Remove it from the oven and set aside to cool, then break it up into big chunks.

Quarter the apples, then put them in a bowl. Cover them with the remaining salt and leave for 20 minutes. Rinse the apples and pat them dry with kitchen paper. (Try to remove as much moisture as possible.)

Pour the oil into a deep-fat fryer or deep-sided saucepan and heat to 180°C/350°F, or until a cube of bread browns in one minute. Add a few apples at a time, frying for 2–3 minutes, or until crispy. Drain on kitchen paper.

To serve, sprinkle the apples with salt and serve in a bowl with the scratchings roughly broken up.

Apple, Tomato and Ginger Chutney

Preparation time: 1 hour 30 minutes
Makes 5 x 250 g/8 oz jars

5 jam jars
1 kg/2 lb red tomatoes
3 green apples (such as Granny Smith)
3 onions, peeled and roughly chopped
3 garlic cloves, peeled and finely chopped
5 cm/2 in fresh ginger, peeled and finely grated
300 g/10 oz sultanas
200 g/7 oz soft brown sugar
freshly ground black pepper and sea salt
600 ml/1 pint white wine vinegar

Preheat the oven to 160°C/325°F/gas mark 3. Wash the jam jars in hot, soapy water until entirely clean, then place them on a baking sheet and put in the oven for 10 minutes. Keep warm before the jam is ready.

Roughly chop the tomatoes, removing any white core, then put them in a large, heavy saucepan. Peel, core and roughly chop the apples. Add them to the pan along with the onions, garlic, ginger, sultanas and brown sugar. Season well with sea salt and black pepper. Pour in half the vinegar. Bring to the boil, then reduce to a simmer and simmer for 40 minutes until the vegetables and apples are tender.

Pour in the remaining white wine vinegar and simmer for a further 30 minutes, or until the chutney is very thick. Stir as necessary to prevent sticking. Check the seasoning and adjust if necessary.

Using a small ladle, fill the warm, sterilized jars with chutney to within 1 cm/½ inch of the top, then wipe them clean. Put a disc of waxed paper wax side down on top of the chutney and seal the jars with airtight lids. Leave to cool, then label and store in a cool, dark, dry place for at least 1 month before serving. It will keep for up to a year.

Scrumpy Jack Cider Gravy

Preparation time: 25 minutes
Serves 6

25–50 g/1–2 oz plain flour
450 ml/¾ pint bottle of Scrumpy Jack dry cider
200 ml/7 fl oz fresh stock, or juices from the roast meat
50 g/2 oz unsalted butter, chilled and cubed
freshly ground black pepper and sea salt

Remove your meat from the roasting tin and wrap in foil, then let it rest.

Pour the juices into a jug, leaving the fat behind. Add the flour to the fat in the roasting tin, stirring it in, and set on the hob over a medium heat. Cook the flour, stirring constantly with a wooden spoon and loosening the residue from the bottom of the tray. Remove from the heat and slowly add the cider. Return to the heat and bring to the boil, stirring. When the gravy starts to thicken, add the stock or reserved juices from the roasting tin. Bring to the boil and boil until the gravy is thick. Remove from the heat and whisk in the butter, a chunk at a time. Season with freshly ground black pepper and sea salt to taste and pour into a warm jug.

Apple, Apricot and Cranberry Stuffing

Preparation time: 1 hour 10 minutes, plus 2 hours steeping time
Serves 4–6

butter, for greasing
100 g/3½ oz dried apple
100 g/3½ oz dried apricots
100 g/3½ oz dried cranberries
100 ml/3½ fl oz clear apple juice
25 ml/1 fl oz olive oil
1 large onion, peeled and chopped
1 garlic clove, peeled and crushed
2 celery sticks, trimmed and chopped
1 apple, peeled, cored and chopped
2 sprigs of fresh thyme
6 fresh sage leaves, chopped
200 g/7 oz cooked chestnuts, roughly chopped
6–8 good butcher's sausages
small handful of fresh flat-leaf parsley, roughly chopped
freshly ground black pepper and sea salt

Preheat the oven to 180°C/350°F/gas mark 4. Butter and season an 18 x 27 cm/1 litre ovenproof dish.

Roughly chop the dried apple and apricots, then put them in a bowl with the cranberries and pour over the apple juice. Cover and leave for about 2 hours, stirring now and again.

Heat the oil in a frying pan and fry the onion, garlic, celery, apple, thyme and sage until soft and melting. Add the chestnuts and the soaked fruits and cook for a further 3–4 minutes. Remove from the heat and leave to cool. Remove the thyme.

Remove the sausages from their skins and put the sausagemeat in a bowl. Add the parsley and the fruit mixture and mix until thoroughly combined. Season well.

Spoon the mixture into the dish and smooth the top. Bake in the oven for 40 minutes, or until cooked in the centre and golden on top.

Whether you are in the mood for something sweet or savoury, there are apple accompaniments for every meal and every appetite. Jewel-like jams for those with a sweet tooth, ginger-spiced chutney to partner a slice or two of cheese and apple sauce to accompany cold cuts of pork or game.

Apple juice comes into its own when it comes to making drinks and smoothies. Apple, Peach and Passionfruit Smoothies are speedy to make and irresisitibly moreish and a glass or two of Apple Mojito – cut through with the taste of fresh mint leaves – is ideal for hot summer days. Apple, Rooibos, Lemon Grass and Mint Iced Tea helps you wind down at the end of a long day and Hot Apple Punch will get you in the party spirit. Try mixing apple juice with other fruit and see what flavours you like best.

Apple Juice

Preparation time: 5 minutes
Makes 1 litre/1¾ pints

1 kg/2 lb organic apples (such as Cox's)
juice of 3 lemons

Cut the apples into wedges, removing the core. Chop the wedges into chunks that are small enough to fit easily through the top of your juicer.

With the motor running, push the chunks into the juicer, then stir in the lemon juice.

Pour the apple juice into a sterilized, airtight bottle and store in the fridge for up to 2 days.

Apple, Peach and Passionfruit Smoothie

Preparation time: 8 minutes
Makes 6 x 300 ml/½ pint glasses

6 ripe peaches
4 passionfruit
200 ml/7 fl oz fresh apple juice
500 ml/17 fl oz natural yogurt
crushed ice
peach wedges, to decorate

Put the peaches in a bowl and pour over boiling water. Leave for up to 1 minute. Drain, and when cool enough to handle, peel off the skin. Cut the fruit in half and remove the stones. Cut the passionfruit in half, spoon the insides into a sieve and, using the back of a spoon, press the juice into a bowl. Discard the seeds.

Put the peaches, passion fruit juice, apple juice and yogurt in a food processor and whizz until smooth. Pour into tall glasses, decorate with peach wedges and serve immediately.

Apple, Cucumber and Beetroot Juice

Preparation time: 5 minutes
Makes 2 x 300 ml/½ pint glasses

4 organic apples (such as Cox's)
1 organic cucumber
2 organic cooked beetroot
ice cubes, to serve

Chop the apples, cucumber and beetroot into chunks that will fit through the top of the juicer. With the motor running, push the chunks through the juicer. Half fill cold glasses with ice and pour in the juice. Serve immediately.

Hot Apple Punch

Preparation time: 8 minutes, plus 2–3 hours infusion time
Makes 1.8 litres/3 pints

4 large unwaxed oranges
6–8 whole cloves
1.5 litre/2½ pints fresh cloudy apple juice
2 cinnamon sticks, roughly broken
100 g/3½ oz quince jelly
100 ml/3½ fl oz Calvados

Cut 2 oranges in half and push the cloves into the halves. Juice the other 2 oranges. Pour the juice into a large saucepan, then add the orange halves, apple juice, cinnamon and quince jelly. Heat gently stirring to dissolve the quince jelly. Remove the pan from the heat and leave to let the flavours infuse for 2–3 hours.

Just before serving, add the Calvados and warm through. Pour into warm glasses and serve.

Apple, Rooibos, Lemon Grass and Mint Iced Tea

Preparation time: 5 minutes, plus 1 hour infusion time
Makes 1.5 litres/2½ pints

2 Rooibos teabags
750 ml/1¼ pint boiling water
2 lemon grass sticks, halved and bruised
handful of fresh mint
750 ml/1¼ pints fresh clear apple juice
ice and fresh mint leaves, to serve

Put the teabags in a large heatproof jug and pour in the boiling water. Leave the teabags for 6–8 minutes, then remove them and add the lemon grass and mint to the jug.

Leave the tea to infuse for 1 hour, then strain it into a large jug. Pour in the apple juice and chill until needed.

To serve, half fill the jug with ice and mint. Pour in the apple tea and serve.

Apple Mojito

Preparation time: 8 minutes
Serves 2

bunch of fresh mint
100 g/3½ oz caster sugar
2 limes, quartered
600 ml/1 pint cloudy apple juice
crushed ice

Remove the leaves from the mint, put them in a jug and add the sugar. Cut the limes into quarters and put into the jug. Using the end of a rolling pin, crush the mint and lime with the sugar.

Spoon the mint mixture into two 400 ml/14 fl oz tall glasses and spoon some crushed ice into each glass. Pour in the apple juice, give a good stir and serve.

Index

First published in 2004 by Conran Octopus Limited,
a part of Octopus Publishing Group,
2–4 Heron Quays, London E14 4JP
www.conran-octopus.co.uk

Publishing Director: Lorraine Dickey
Senior Editor: Katey Day
Art Director: Chi Lam
Design: Carl Hodson
Photography: David Loftus
Stylist: Harriet Docker
Production Manager: Angela Couchman
Home Economy: Louise Mackaness
Apple dish from Nicola Harris Design, SA.

British Cataloguing-in-Publication Data.
A catalogue record for this book is available from
the British Library

ISBN 1 84091 404 1

To order please ring Conran Octopus Direct
on 01903 828503

Printed and bound in China

Author's Acknowledgements
Oliver, Sarah and Jono, many thanks for putting up with
me at Christmas! Harriet, as ever you have been fantastic.
Finally a very BIG thank you to David for all your help.